AIR VANGUARD 2

REPUBLIC F-105 THUNDERCHIEF

PETER DAVIES

First published in Great Britain in 2012 by Osprey Publishing,
Midland House, West Way, Botley, Oxford, OX2 0PH, UK
44–02 23rd St, Suite 219, Long Island City, NY 11101, USA

A CIP catalog record for this book is available from the British Library

Print ISBN: 978 1 78096 173 6
PDF e-book ISBN: 978 1 78096 174 3
EPUB e-book ISBN: 978 1 78096 175 0

Index by Zoe Ross
Typeset in Deca Sans and Sabon
Originated by PDQ Digital Media Solutions Ltd, Suffolk UK
Printed in China through Bookbuilders

12 13 14 15 16 10 9 8 7 6 5 4 3 2 1

www.ospreypublishing.com

Osprey Publishing is supporting the Woodland Trust, the UK's leading
woodland conservation charity, by funding the dedication of trees.

ACKNOWLEDGMENTS

I am most grateful to the following for their kind assistance with this
book: Lt Col Bob Cooley, USAF (Ret), Col Ben Fuller, USAF (Ret), Col
Robert Gobble, USAF (Ret), Col Bill Hosmer, USAF (Ret), Lt Col Warren
Kerzon, USAF (Ret), Col William Kriz, USAF (Ret), Lt Col Barry A. Miller,
USAF (Ret), Lt Col Ronald Soule, USAF (Ret), Col Boyd L. Van Horn,
USAF (Ret).

GLOSSARY

AAA antiaircraft artillery

AFCS automatic flight control system

AFRES Air Force Reserve

AMI airspeed/Mach indicator

ANG Air National Guard

ATI Applied Technology Inc

AVVI altitude vertical velocity indicator

CAP combat air patrol

CBU cluster bomb unit

CCTS combat crew training squadron

CCTW combat crew training wing

CEP circular error of probability (accuracy of dropped ordnance)

EWO electronic warfare officer

FAC forward air control

Fan Song Soviet radar unit for guiding surface-to-air missiles.

GCA ground-controlled approach

GOR general operating requirement

KIA killed in action

LABS low-altitude bombing system ("toss" bombing)

MER multiple ejection rack

ORI operational readiness inspection

PACAF Pacific Air Forces

PAL permissive action link

PCS permanent change of station

RAT ram-air turbine

ResCAP rescue combat air patrol

RHAW radar homing and warning

RP6 Route Pack 6. The north-eastern section of North Vietnam, one of
several 'packs' allocated for USAF air operations

RTAFB Royal Thai Air Force Base

RTU replacement training unit

SAC Strategic Air Command (bombers on short-notice nuclear alert)

SAM surface-to-air missile

SEAD suppression of enemy air defenses

SEE-SAMS sense, exploit and evade surface-to-air missile system.

SVAF South Vietnamese Air Force

TAC Tactical Air Command

TACAN tactical air navigation

TDY temporary deployment

TFS tactical fighter squadron

TFW tactical fighter wing

TOT time on target

USAFE US Air Forces, Europe

VFR visual flight rules

VPAF Vietnamese Peoples' Air Force

WSC Weapons System Concept

CONTENTS

REPUBLIC F-105 THUNDERCHIEF

INTRODUCTION

Fighter aircraft development in the 1950s might be summarized as "faster, higher and (inevitably) more expensive." Designers, using dramatic advances in power-plant technology and aerodynamics, took the top speed of fighters from 600mph for the 1950 F-86A Sabre to 1,606mph for the F4H-1 Phantom II at the end of that decade. The latter was also zoom-climbed to 98,447ft, more than twice the service ceiling of the F-86A. For bombers too, the performance increases were spectacular. While a 1950 Korean War Boeing B-29 Superfortress cruised at 220mph, the delta-wing Convair B-58A Hustler nuclear bomber was capable of Mach 2.2 and reached a combat ceiling of 63,000ft, almost double that of the B-29.

With a steady reduction in the size of the atomic weapons that were the bedrock of US defense strategy in the 1950s, it became possible to combine fighter and bomber capability in a single, high-performance aircraft. The 10,000lb Mk II "Fat Man" nuclear bomb of 1945 had given way by 1960 to the B57 Mod 1 weapon weighing only 500lbs, but with the same 20 kilotons explosive force. It could be hung beneath fighters such as the Republic F-84F Thunderstreak, adding a second, tactical battlefield level of nuclear deterrence to the dominant might of Strategic Air Command's huge intercontinental bomber force, which, flying at high altitudes, had become vulnerable to Soviet surface-to-air missiles. Development of "dog-fighting" air superiority fighters was curtailed and limited numbers of missile-launching interceptors, including the Convair F-102 and F-106, were bought to defend the USA against Soviet nuclear bombers. Existing interceptor designs like the North American F-100 Super Sabre and McDonnell F-101 Voodoo were reconfigured as nuclear-capable strike aircraft.

The F-105's ancestor, the P-47 Thunderbolt, was unquestionably one of the greatest of World War II fighters, flying more than half a million missions, destroying more than 12,000 enemy aircraft with a 4.6 to 1 success rate, and dropping 132,482 tons of bombs. Like the F-105 it was tough, heavy (19,400lbs maximum compared with 6,675lbs for a Spitfire V), and reliable. (Republic Aviation)

The Republic F-105, making its first flight halfway through the 1950s, was purpose-built for this scenario. It was the biggest, heaviest and most powerful fighter of its day, designed to fly a straight course with an internally carried nuclear bomb and limited all-weather radar and all-weather navigation/

attack avionics to strike tactical targets deep inside enemy territory. Traditional air-to-air fighting ability was minimized; the F-105 relied on speed to evade enemy interceptors. Thunderchiefs stood ready in Europe, Japan, and the USA to fly such missions throughout most of the 1960s, but the aircraft's secure place in aviation history was earned in totally different circumstances.

President Lyndon B. Johnson's decision to respond to North Vietnamese gunboat attacks on US naval vessels in the Gulf of Tonkin involved Far East Air Force F-105 units from August 1964 in retaliatory strikes. F-105s were to fly combat missions over Vietnam and Laos until the final stages of the conflict in 1974. They were the most potent tactical weapons available in the area in 1964, when elements within the US military briefly considered a nuclear response to North Vietnam's aggressive stance.

However, an increasing campaign of tactical strikes required formations of F-105s to fly conventional bombing missions against inconspicuous targets in the Laotian jungle and then against larger military and industrial targets in Hanoi and Haiphong (situated within the world's most heavily defended airspace) in North Vietnam from March 1965 in Operation *Rolling Thunder*. Rather than flying straight-and-level nuclear attacks, the heavily laden F-105s had to maneuver strenuously to avoid enemy gunfire and ground-to-air missiles. Although their original nuclear role did not envisage air-to-air opposition, F-105s over North Vietnam were attacked by MiG fighters more frequently than any other American aircraft. Their pilots succeeded in shooting down at least 27.5 MiG-17s in 18 months at the height of *Rolling Thunder*.

Single-seat F-105Ds and many of the two-seat F-105Fs originally built as conversion trainers flew more than 20,000 combat missions by the war's end, but some of these were conducted by modified F-105Fs that introduced a new type of air war for the USAF. Equipped with electronic countermeasures equipment, they detected and destroyed the Russian-supplied surface-to-air missile (SAM) sites that presented a major threat to US aircraft. The price of using the F-105 as the primary strike and anti-SAM fighter over the North was high. More than 330 Thunderchiefs were lost, and although this represented only 1.6 aircraft for every thousand sorties flown, such heavy overall utilization reduced the F-105 force by 1972 to only 264 (including 45 non-combat F-105Bs) out of the total production of 833. Surviving battle-worn examples were reassigned to nine Air National Guard and USAF Reserve units from 1971, and some continued in service until May 1983.

First flown in 1952, the F-84F Thunderstreak was a swept-wing development of the Korean War stalwart F-84B, with a license-built British Armstrong-Siddeley Sapphire (J65) engine developing about a quarter of the power of the F-105's J75 turbojet, but enabling it to reach 658mph and to carry a nuclear weapon. Like other Republic fighters, it needed plenty of runway. (Republic Aviation)

The RF-84F Thunderflash was the basis of the original AP-63-FBX design that evolved into the F-105. Its intake configuration was echoed in the first two YF-105As but its much more slender fuselage reflects the comparatively small housing and fuel appetite of the J65 compared with the F-105's massive, afterburning J75. (Fairchild-Hiller)

DESIGN AND DEVELOPMENT

The Kartveli Heritage

When the Republic Aviation Company submitted its APX-63-FBX design to the USAF in February 1952 for an aircraft that became the F-105 Thunderchief, it drew upon considerable experience in producing tough, reliable fighters. Founded in 1939 from the Seversky Aircraft Corporation, it employed visionary designer Alex Kartveli, who had fought in World War I, supported his degree studies by working as a trapeze artist and teaching maths, and worked for the

Alexander Kartveli worked on this futuristic XF-103 proposal four years before the initial F-105 drawings were made. Its 37,000lb thrust XJ67 turbojet/ramjet occupied half the titanium and stainless steel fuselage, driving the 40,000lb aircraft at 2,600mph. The forward fuselage housed radar, a pilot with a periscope, and six Falcon missiles. (Fairchild Republic Company)

Fokker/Atlantic Aircraft Company after emigrating to America. His single-seat fighter designs as chief engineer for fellow Russian emigrant Alexander de Seversky evolved into Kartveli's first masterpiece, the P-47 Thunderbolt, the heaviest single-engined fighter of World War II and one of the most successful. More than 15,000 were ordered, and they gave the USAAF and many other air forces an excellent air-to-air fighter that could also deliver ground-attack ordnance with bombs or rockets.

Its successor, the 1946 F-84 Thunderjet, was Kartveli's first jet-powered fighter. It became an effective fighter-bomber during the Korean War and later versions introduced the low-altitude bombing system (LABS) with tactical nuclear weapons and in-flight refueling. It was the USAF's last fighter with unswept wings, and by 1949 Kartveli's team was working on a much faster successor with 40 degrees wing sweep, the F-84F Thunderstreak. More than 2,700 of these very capable nuclear strike fighters equipped seven Tactical Air Command (TAC) fighter-bomber groups and flew with ten other nations' air forces. Its photo-reconnaissance derivative, the RF-84F Thunderflash, with a lengthened camera-carrying nose requiring the air intakes to be moved to the wing-roots, was in some ways the direct predecessor of the F-105.

Kartveli's designers worked on other highly innovative projects such as the turboprop-powered XF-84H, the jet- and rocket-driven XF-91 Thunderceptor (the first American combat aircraft to go supersonic in level flight), and the extraordinary missile-like XF-103. Built of stainless steel and titanium, the latter interceptor combined turbojet and ramjet power and was intended to reach Mach 4, armed with six Falcon air-to-air missiles and 36 air-to-air rockets. Burgeoning costs and power-plant delays led to its cancellation in 1957 after nine years' effort.

In 1950 Kartveli had begun work on a supersonic, all-weather tactical fighter-bomber while his F-84F was still approaching prototype completion. It began life as an F-84 derivative with an internal weapons bay to hold two Mk 28 lightweight nuclear bombs, eliminating the drag of an externally carried weapon then used on TAC fighters. A much more powerful engine was required to compensate for the increased structural weight and to give significant performance improvement. At the time most jet aircraft suffered from lack of power, but a new generation of engines including the Bristol Olympus (as the J67) and Pratt and Whitney's innovative J57 (used in several other Century Series fighters) offered up to 16,000lbs of thrust with afterburning, compared with 7,800lbs for the J65 engine used for Kartveli's RF-84F. Two parallel designs, the F-84X with a J57 and new wing, and the AP-63-FBX, occupied Republic's drawing boards in 1951. The latter, derived

The second YF-105A, with straight, subsonic RF-84F-style intakes, the small vertical tail, and uncontoured fuselage of the first two aircraft. 54-0099 lacked the four-petal airbrakes that had appeared on the first prototype. It was used for testing at Edwards AFB until February 24, 1960. (Republic Aviation)

from the RF-84F, had a 3ft fuselage extension, a similar but enlarged wing, General Electric J73 engine (later replaced by an Allison J71), internal bomb bay and a top speed of 800kts. The AP-63 proposal rather than the more conventional F-84X was favored by the USAF after its February 1952 submission and was given the F-105 designation.

Weapons System Concept

Between the awarding of the initial contract for 199 F-105As in September 1952 and the first flight of the YF-105A prototype three years later, the design underwent considerable development and uncertainty. Republic's deal was of a new type. The Korean War, continued until July 1953, had revealed unexpected advances in Soviet aircraft design that accelerated America's desire to restore its previous technological lead. Acquiring supersonic fighters became an urgent requirement, and improved program management was seen as a way of imposing greater speed and efficiency on the procurement of new hardware. The increasing complexity of military aircraft meant that producing an airframe was only part of a research and manufacturing process that also involved radar and avionics, powerplant, armament and the machine tools, and metals to build those products, as well as the equipment required to sustain the aircraft in service use.

In all those fields unprecedented advances were being made in the early 1950s, although there were several cases where projects were canceled because an engine or radar had failed to meet its ambitious deadlines. Managing all these diverse elements under a Weapons System Concept (WSC) gave one manager (usually the airframe manufacturer) overall control, and one of the first aircraft to be included in the program, the F-105, became Weapons System WS-306.

Republic Aviation managed the entire project, including the integration of the proposed Allison J71 engine into a fighter that was expected to reach Mach 1.5 with a nuclear weapons load. One of the original 108 preliminary outline designs used two J71s to attain this speed. A March 20, 1953 contract amendment reflected the end of the demands engendered by the Korean War in reducing the original order to 37 aircraft. The company continued development work, hoping for more orders, although only an additional batch of nine RF-105s (very sophisticated night/all-weather reconnaissance versions with moving-target-indicating radar, infrared sensors, and partly automated navigation equipment) was appended to the contract in September 1953.

As the design matured, the RF-84F-style all-moving stabilator was moved from its position on the tailfin to the base of the lower fuselage, like the North

F-105B-5-RE 54-0109 demonstrates an early production configuration, with extended refueling probe, lack of small rear-view windows behind the canopy, and an open bomb bay. Used at Eglin AFB for testing, it ended its days in 1965 as a GJF-105B ground-instructional airframe. (USAF)

American F-100, to keep it effectively within the airflow at high angles of attack. The thin wing was moved to a mid-fuselage position and swept to 45 degrees (also like the F-100) and a four-piece "clover leaf" airbrake was added to the rear fuselage behind the jet efflux. An enlarged internal bomb bay could take a 3,400lb nuclear weapon or, for conventional bombing missions, a 2,000lb bomb or an additional fuel tank. Originally, four wing-mounted T-130 0.60cal machine guns were specified, but the quest for common armament in US combat aircraft persuaded the design team to incorporate a General Electric T-171 (later M61A1) rotary cannon in the nose instead. Importantly for the F-105's combat future, there were four under-wing ordnance hard-points.

Once again, engine development delays arose, and it became clear that the Allison J71 would be late and below the required thrust specification. Republic reverted to the J57 as an interim engine. A further problem, common to most fighter designs of the day, was creeping weight increase as further additions were specified by the customer. This and the uncertainty over the engine prompted the USAF to suspend the WS-306A project at the end of 1953. It had the F-100 and F-104 Starfighter for fighter duties, and the YF-105A strike fighter had a lower priority after the end of hostilities in Korea. Republic had attempted to adapt their baseline, relatively simple AP-63 into the advanced fighter-bomber/reconnaissance vehicle that the Air Force now needed, but this involved them in many innovative areas of aviation technology where the risks were considerable and delays or failure were strong possibilities.

However, the project continued and the company accelerated its quest for a power-plant solution, finally settling on the YJ75 that Pratt & Whitney were building for the F-106 Delta Dart. It offered an unprecedented 23,000lbs of thrust but it wasn't ready, so when the project was eventually revived in February 1954 Pratt & Whitney's well-tried J57 had to be specified for the first ten aircraft. USAF faith in the project still remained tentative and a drastic cut allowing only three aircraft, all with the J57, was made in September 1954, only six months ahead of the original delivery date for production aircraft. Finally, in December 1954 the USAF issued a general operating requirement (GOR-49) that fitted the description of the J75-powered F-105. Usually, the manufacturers produced designs to meet pre-ordained GORs, but this decision reversed that process somewhat and reflected the USAF's renewed interest in more advanced tactical strike capability. The requirement included a new MA-8 fire-control system, in-flight refueling and a revised in-service date extended by three years to 1958. Two J57-powered prototype YF-105As

 F-105D-25-RE 60-0421 "The Great Pumpkin" of the 469th TFS, 388th TFW, Korat RTAFB, Thailand, May 13, 1966

Before official squadron tail-codes were applied at Korat in 1966, the drab camouflage made aircraft within a flight of F-105s difficult to identify visually. This squadron experimented with individual identity letters (in this case "P" for Pumpkin) while others used World War II-style symbols such as a triangle. The 469th TFS was allocated JV codes in 1968. This aircraft's bomb load of six 750lb M117s was fairly standard throughout the war. It also carries an ALQ-71 ECM pod and two 450-gallon external fuel tanks. "Snoopy" cartoon figures were among the most popular sources of nose-art during the Vietnam War.

The third prototype North American F-107A 55-120, with a semi-recessed fuel tank that could be replaced by a TX-28 nuclear store. This aircraft was handed over to NACA to test a side-stick controller, later used in the North American X-15 experimental aircraft. After 40 flights it was badly damaged in a takeoff accident and scrapped. (North American Aviation)

were ordered on January 19, 1955 with ten YF-105Bs to follow, using the YJ75 turbojet. Interest in the reconnaissance variant (YRF-105B) with nose-mounted cameras remained strong at this stage and three were included in this initial order.

The revised order was placed under another procurement concept, "concurrency," also known as the Cook-Craigie plan. This by-passed the need for a prototype, using the first batch of production aircraft to conduct a flight test program while production continued. Like the WSC, it assumed that the original design would be virtually satisfactory from the outset and that no radical changes would be required throughout the production and service period. Traditionally, a process of trial-and-error testing with numerous, costly prototypes had been normal, but WSC presumed that designers would get it right first time and that quantity production could proceed immediately the design was approved. With Cook-Craigie, any minor modifications could be progressively incorporated in the first production batch and full production could be gradually accelerated as small changes were introduced to achieve the definitive production standard. The first aircraft program under this scheme, the Convair F-102 Delta Dagger interceptor, did require substantial redesign when it was found to be incapable of supersonic speed rather than the intended Mach 1.5, and the definitive production specification was not firmed up until the 66th production aircraft left the factory, although further changes were to come even later. However, WSC and its successors became the standard and generally successful methods of managing a wide range of defense projects.

The Rival

While Republic designers worked on the F-105, North American Aviation were also conceiving a new fighter that they hoped would succeed their well-proven F-100 Super Sabre. Various upgrades to the F-100 to recast it as an F-100BI all-weather interceptor or F-100B fighter-bomber were outlined between 1952 and 1954, but it was a development of the F-100B, the F-107A, that attracted a USAF contract for 33 aircraft (reduced to 12 a month later) on June 11, 1956. Like the F-105, it was an evolutionary design based on a previous success for the company, and it retained the basic wing planform, but with spoilers and slotted flaps in place of the usual flight control surfaces. The vertical tail, similar in appearance to the F-100's but much larger, was a one-piece, all-moving component. The company moved the previous design's nose-mounted air intake to allow for a radar, and for the F-107A the inlet was placed above the fuselage just behind the pilot's canopy. Whereas Republic followed the USAF requirement for an internal bomb bay, North American used a semi-recessed, under-fuselage nuclear "store" or fuel tank plus six wing hard-points for other ordnance totaling 10,000lbs, delivered with an XMA-12 fire-control system. It used the same J75 engine as the F-105, giving it a top speed of at least Mach 2. Despite the potential hazard for the pilot of having to eject close to a yawning air intake, the F-107A was highly regarded by the USAF, and North American, who topped the table of US defense firms, were surprised when the F-105 was selected instead. Whether the F-107A was awarded preliminary development contracts in order to instill a greater sense of urgency into the Republic program, or whether it was just a political decision to provide work for Republic's Farmingdale factory, is debatable. If the aircraft's further development had turned out to be less troubled than the F-105's it could have been in service at about the same time, but the cancellation of the program after over $105m had been spent made the F-100 the last in a highly successful series of USAF fighters to emerge from North American production lines.

After mock-up reviews of the J75 engine in January 1955, it was judged to be suitable for the YF-105, but the first two YF-105As used J57-P-25 with slightly extended exhaust nozzles. In the year between cancellation and revival of the project, Republic had continued to refine the production standard so that testing of the first YF-105A made rapid progress. The first pair of YF-105As retained the RF-84F-style subsonic intakes, and the vertical stabilizer was smaller than the final version, as was the fuselage overall. After completion in September 1955, the first YF-105A (54-0098) was taken to Edwards Air Force Base, ground-tested and flown on October 22 by the company's chief test pilot, Russell Roth. Despite its less powerful engine, the aircraft made a supersonic first flight followed by 12 more flights, leading to its official acceptance by the USAF. On its final flight, a main undercarriage leg extended during a 5.5G turn at around 530kts and was ripped off by the airflow. "Rusty" Roth managed to bring it back to Edwards, but the subsequent hard landing fractured the aircraft's "backbone" and it was apparently scrapped on November 16. The second, very similar, YF-105A was ready to resume the test program by January 28 but the results of both flight tests and wind-tunnel experiments showed clearly that, even with the improved J75 engine, the F-105 was unlikely to reach its intended performance levels due to excessive drag at high speeds.

Richard T. Whitcomb at NACA Langley Aeronautical Laboratory, who later brought greater efficiency to many of the world's commercial aircraft through the invention of "winglets" and the supercritical aerofoil, devised a drag-reduction system known as area rule. By recontouring an aircraft's fuselage so that pressure was distributed over the airframe more evenly, the effects of transonic drag were much reduced. His discovery saved the F-102A Delta Dagger and it brought similar benefits to the F-105. Like the F-102A and several other aircraft of the time, the Republic design was given a "Coke bottle" fuselage profile, although Kartveli found this excessive and had it reduced. Fuselage length was increased by almost 2ft (which also allowed room for a larger radar) and the vertical stabilizer was heightened by 2ft and increased in area by over 30 percent, with an air intake at its base to cool the engine

JF-105B-2-RE 54-0112/JF-3 shows the nose contours of the RF-105B prototypes with the camera ports covered over. Its nose was filled with test instrumentation and rearward-looking cameras were attached just behind the "FH-112" buzz number to film stores separation in flight, in this case rocket pods. (Author's collection)

This F-105B-20-RE (57-5836) in TAC markings tests a 26-bomb load, including two multiple ejection racks on special adapters to attach them to the fuselage. The barrels of its M61 gun are visible through the gun-port in the nose. This aircraft later flew with the New Jersey ANG until March 1974. (USAF)

compartment. The size increase was a response to earlier difficulties with other contemporary designs, such as the F-100A, where inadequate directional stability at high speed had caused losses. As a precaution, the area of the ventral fin was also increased to maintain stability at high angles of attack and the horizontal stabilizer was strengthened.

One of the F-105's most distinctive features, its swept-forward air intakes, was also added at this stage. Derived by Antonio Ferri from work on the XF-103 interceptor, the intakes performed far better than the original type at high speeds. They included moveable "plugs" to change the cross-section of the intake and match the airflow to the engine's requirements at varying flight speeds. The plugs and associated internal bleed-air doors were controlled by the aircraft's Bendix central air data computer (CADC).

These redesigned features delayed the flight of the third F-105 until May 26, 1956 and caused a redesignation as YF-105B. The J75 engine was in place from March 14, 1956 onwards, as were the four "petal" airbrakes that could be opened for dive-bombing or as air brakes on landing using the two side elements. The first F-105B-1-RE (54-0100) made its maiden flight at Edwards AFB on May 26, 1956, although test pilot Henry Beaird couldn't persuade the nose landing gear to extend for landing. He made a wheels-up landing with minimal damage, but the recovery crane driver dropped the aircraft a foot above the dry lakebed where Beaird had landed it, causing far more severe damage. The following month the USAF received Republic's request to name the aircraft "Thunderchief" and approved the choice on July 25. In the same month the three RF-105s, which were nearing completion at Republic's factory in Farmingdale, New York, were canceled in favor of McDonnell's RF-101

B

1. F-105B-15-RE 57-5793, 335th TFS, 4th TFW, late 1959
2. F-105D-25-RE 61-0163, 562nd TFS, 23rd TFW, 1964
3. F-105D-6-RE 60-0422 "The Red Baron," 469th TFS, 388th TFW, Korat RTAFB, 1967
4. F-105D-30-RE 62-4246 "Thor's Hammer," 357th TFS, 355th TFW, Takhli RTAFB

1   75793
U.S. AIR FORCE
FH-793

2   10163
U.S. AIR FORCE
FH-163A

3   USAF
00422

4   RU
246
Thor's Hammer

F-105B-10-REs of Detachment 1 of the 335th TFS during the type's Category II trials at Eglin AFB, Florida, in 1959, surrounded by maintainers who struggled to keep pace with the constant modifications. The F-105's traditional round cockpit dials can be seen in "FH-779," later assigned to the New Jersey ANG until 1975. (Republic Aviation)

Voodoo and redesignated JF-105Bs for USAF flight-test duties for ordnance carriage and jettison methods and to develop the autopilot system.

The second F-105B wasn't accepted until December 1956 and it too made a belly-landing. Test pilot Lindell Hendrix brought it back from a January 30, 1957 check flight to find that the undercarriage would not extend. It was later realized that auxiliary air intakes in the main gear wheel wells remained open when the landing gear retracted, causing enough suction to prevent the units from lowering. Changes to the air by-pass ducting cured this expensive quirk.

With the airframe configuration apparently settled, attention turned to the aircraft's all-weather bombing system, Weapons System 306A. This included a General Electric FC-5 flight-control system and autopilot, a Bendix CADC, and MA-8 fire-control system. From July 1957, the lightweight AN/APN-105 Doppler navigation system was also cleared for use in the F-105 from F-105B-15-RE 57-5785 onwards, with nine earlier aircraft receiving it as a retrofit. The first 15 F-105s were all used to test the new aircraft under both tropical and arctic conditions for combat evaluation and for static-load tests in addition to proving the very advanced General Electric XMA-8 system. Republic announced that one-third of the cost of each aircraft was for its electronic systems, among the 65,000 separate items that made up an F-105B. The aircraft's performance, evaluated in June 1957, still showed that supersonic acceleration above Mach 1.8 was below requirements. The USAF also issued a list of weapons that the aircraft would carry, ranging from TX-38 and TX-43 nuclear bombs to AIM-9 Sidewinder missiles and ALE-2 chaff pods. Even at this early stage an ECM pod was included. Overall, the Air Force Flight Test center judged that the F-105B "has the potential of becoming an excellent fighter-bomber." Several of these test aircraft survived to become ground-instructional airframes or museum occupants, though one (54-0106) was lost with Republic's chief test pilot, Martin J. Signiorelli, over the Atlantic near New York in unexplained circumstances on December 16, 1959. It was the first fatal accident in the program.

The company-designed ejection seat was ground-tested in June 1958 and found to be effective in near zero-altitude, zero-speed conditions, but a more powerful M-3 catapult was specified to prevent the seat from hitting the vertical tailfin in ejections at supersonic speed. Several pilots were to find that modification a lifesaver in Vietnam. A change to the cockpit canopy was made from the fifth aircraft onwards, deleting the small rearward-vision transparencies that were part of its RF-84F/AP-63 heritage. The manually operated canopy with a single hinge-point at its upper rear edge was replaced by an electrical unit that required two larger hinges at each side of the fuselage, removing the limited rear-view possibilities. From Block 20 onwards an arresting hook was added beneath the rear fuselage, while other early production batches added antiskid brakes, cartridge starting for the engine, and a double-sized oxygen system.

In order to make up some of the three-year delay in introducing the F-105 to service use, it was decided to conduct the second stage of its operational test and evaluation (OT&E Category II) within the first USAF unit to receive the aircraft. Republic handed over the first production aircraft, F-105B-6-RE 54-0111, on May 27, 1958 for the 4th Fighter Day Wing to test at Eglin AFB, although it wasn't officially unveiled to the public until July 28, when it was demonstrated at a show celebrating 50 years of US Army and Air Force cooperation. Briefly redesignated as a JF-105B in July 1958 with the Air Proving Ground Center at Eglin, by August it was decorated with the green nose and tail bands of the Detachment 1, 335th TFS, with the squadron's Indian head design on the tail. The 335th's Fighter Day Squadron description was altered to Tactical Fighter Squadron in recognition of the new fighter's role just before testing began.

Under Lt Col Robert Scott, commander of the 335th TFS "Chiefs," Category II testing proceeded at a slow pace, overrunning its November 30, 1959 deadline by four months. Contributory factors were mainly technical difficulties with so much innovative equipment that was constantly being modified. A decision to use the J75-P-19W engine offering an extra 2,000lbs of water-injected thrust in F-105Bs from Production Block 20 onwards and to retrofit it to earlier aircraft was another source of delay. Project Optimize, instigated late in 1959, was an attempt to bring all F-105Bs up to the same production standard and this too meant many updates to earlier aircraft. Republic received three extensions to their original production deadlines, and at one stage stopped production altogether while awaiting parts to implement Optimize changes on the production line and other successive updates that the USAF demanded. Management of the WSC was proving more of a challenge for Republic's management than its proponents had hoped. Recriminations between the company and Air Force became loud, but both were committed to what they already knew to be an outstanding aircraft. Production recommenced, but it took ten months to make enough F-105Bs to equip the first squadron with 18 aircraft in order to complete the testing, and another 12 months to equip the whole of the 4th TFW at Seymour Johnson AFB. The wing continued to operate its previous F-100 Super Sabre complement in parallel with the new F-105Bs for longer than anticipated, finishing with the former fighter only in mid-1960.

One of the nine F-105Bs assigned to the 4520th Air Demonstration Squadron, the Thunderbirds, in 1964, led by Maj Paul Kattau. Red and blue smoke could be controlled from the control stick grip and throttle, the fuel system was modified for extended inverted flight, a spare drag 'chute was stored in the gun compartment, and a cockpit entry ladder was installed. External tanks were for delivery and transit flights only. (Republic Aviation)

This F-105B-10-RE (57-5776), seen at Nellis AFB in April 1959, was specially marked for the 4th TFW commander, Col Timothy F. O'Keefe, with the wing's badge on a white tail band surrounded by the four squadron colors. (USAF)

Weapons system testing under Category III was still pending in July 1960, and the entire 334th and 335th TFS deployed to Williams AFB, Arizona for the conventional weapons phase. Despite yet more delays caused by spare parts shortages for the still-troublesome MA-8 fire-control systems that were the main focus of the tests, the program was completed on August 15, 1960. The 334th TFS then moved to Eglin AFB, where nuclear weapons delivery qualification took place until December 15, 1960. A final phase took place at Nellis AFB, Nevada in 1961, where all aspects of the F-105B's weapons capability were wrung out. The months of testing had included a demonstration of the F-105B's speed when Brig Gen Joseph H. Moore set a new world speed record of 1,216.48mph (average) over a 100km closed-circuit course in Project Fast Wind at Edwards AFB on December 11, 1959. The following August, Lt Col Scott and Capt Albert Funk flew 1,600 miles from Eglin to George AFB using the F-105Bs' avionics to provide what the Press called "automatic pilotless control" throughout the flight.

With maintenance requirements often approaching 150 manhours for each hour of flight in 1959, and availability rates sometimes dropping below 25 percent, the F-105B's reputation was in need of this favorable publicity, as uncomplimentary nicknames ("Thud," "Squash-bomber," etc.) were beginning to circulate. One of the many satirical comments during the F-105's early service period was that Republic had intended to build it out of concrete, until they found that metal would be heavier. Other witty commentators suggested that the aircraft need not take off to attack its targets, as it could just mow them down during its rather extended takeoff run.

However, the Category II and III trials had shown that it was a stable, well-behaved machine in the air, with no handling eccentricities, and excellent

C

1. F-105F-1-RE 63-8327 "Sweet Caroline," 44th TFS, 355th TFW, Takhli RTAFB, summer 1970

2. F-105D-10-RE 60-0458, 563rd TFS, 23rd TFW, McConnell AFB, April 1971

3. F-105G-1-RE, 63-8316, 17th WWS, 388th TFW, Korat RTAFB, January 1973

4. F-105D-31-RE 62-4353 "No Guts, No Glory," 466th TFS, 419th TFW, Hill AFB Utah, July 1982

1

2

3

4

A 335th TFS maintainer carefully maneuvers an MJ-1 weapons loader bearing an M61A1 "Vulcan" cannon for one of the squadron's F-105Bs. The gun could fire up to 89 rounds per second in a virtually continuous stream. The gun first appeared in 1956 in the Lockheed F-104A Starfighter and soon became the standard US aircraft gun. (USAF)

accuracy in ordnance delivery and gunnery. It was still not the all-weather attacker that the USAF really wanted though, and after 75 F-105Bs had been built it was followed by the definitive, all-weather F-105D. Development work on the F-105D began with the USAF's November 1957 decision to use the AN/ASG-19 Thunderstick fire-control system as the bombing and navigation "brain" to provide visual or blind ordnance delivery and air-to-air gun and missile modes. It was linked to a new Autonetics NASARR R-14A radar that required a bigger radome than the F-105B's limited E-34 ranging radar, which resulted in the repositioning of the M61A1 cannon further back in the fuselage. In the cockpit some of the key instruments presented information on easily read vertical tape bars rather than the traditional round "steam gauges" of the F-105B. The revised F-105 was approved in March 1958, and by May the USAF had ordered 383 F-105Ds and 89 two-seat versions, known initially as the F-105E.

The additional equipment's extra weight necessitated stronger landing gear and brakes, while the inclusion of the more powerful J75-P-19W engine needed some redesign of the rear fuselage to accommodate its power-boosting water injection system and reservoir. Reconfiguration of the air intakes' internal geometry and size was also required for the extra thrust. The rest of the airframe was substantially unchanged, but Republic asserted that the alterations would mean a longer construction time for each F-105D: 214 work-days per unit compared with 144 for an F-105B. In an effort to recoup the extra costs, a USAF board recommended deleting the M61 gun, the ALE-2 chaff dispenser, and the ability to carry ALQ-31 ECM pods, as well as the APS-54 radar warning receiver and the explosive suppression system for the fuel tanks. Fortunately for F-105 pilots in Vietnam most of these cuts were avoided, although the lack of fuel tank explosive suppression meant the fuel tanks had to be replaced by self-sealing versions with internal polyurethane foam to improve crash resistance after numerous combat losses.

The first F-105D (58-1146) flew on June 9, 1959 with Lin Hendrix at the helm. An intensive test program revealed persistent problems with the J75-P-19W engine and ASG-19 fire-control system, the latter requiring three special programs culminating in Project Black Box to rationalize all the small updates to the system. The 335th TFS was an obvious choice to conduct Category II tests at Eglin AFB, and these took place between the end of December 1960 and October 31, 1961. The squadron then returned to its Seymour Johnson AFB home base on November 22, 1961 to conduct Category III tests, having proved the F-105D's systems to be less troublesome than those in the F-105B, although the ASG-19 could still be temperamental in hot and humid conditions, as later experience in Thailand was to show. The lengthy test program, on top of the delays with the F-105B, was essential, as the USAF plans in early 1961 involved 14 Tactical Air Command (TAC) wings of F-105Ds. The delivery of the first operational F-105D to the 4520th Combat Crew Training Wing at Nellis AFB in March 1961 was the beginning of this massive reequipment operation.

TECHNICAL SPECIFICATIONS

Airframe

Fuselage
The F-105's basic structure was essentially an evolutionary development of the airframes used for the company's jet fighters from the 1946 XP-84 onwards. The semi-monocoque fuselage was manufactured in four sections. The nose section included a pressurized cockpit, avionics, the T171 (M61) gun with its ammunition supply, and the nose-wheel bay. A center section enclosed fuel tanks and the internal weapons bay (almost 16ft long and 32in in depth) with two inward-opening doors that were cleared for use up to Mach 2. At the time, it was the only single-seat fighter with an internal bomb bay. Two large frames took the main aerodynamic load of the wings, which were attached at this point. The aft section behind the wing housed the J75 engine and more fuel tanks. The rear fuselage, complete with vertical and horizontal stabilizers, was detachable (as it was on many single-engined jet aircraft at the time) to facilitate maintenance. At its rear end were the four "petals" of the air brake, used to slow the aircraft for a subsonic diving weapons delivery or for the pilot to eject safely at speeds below 550kts (200kts at above 2,000ft were the recommended ejection conditions).

Although the structure was relatively conventional, Republic engineers were innovative in using panels that were milled to the exact thickness needed at each area of the airframe to provide the necessary strength and rigidity. Although much more expensive, this process saved weight.

Wing and Undercarriage
The wing, 385ft in area, used two main aluminum spars running the full length of the structure, with another single structure at right angles to the centerline. It was swept at 45 degrees with 3 degrees anhedral and center-mounted to reduce the "wake" effect of the airflow over the horizontal tailplane. Wing loading for the F-105D was between 127 and 137lbs per square foot depending on the mission configuration. The center-mounted position and the need to provide ground clearance for the magnesium ventral fin necessitated a pair of

very long, inward-retracting Bendix main undercarriage members, giving the F-105 its famous "standing tall" appearance. The distance from the ground to the top of the canopy was 12ft 4in. It also permitted the mounting of heavy bomb loads beneath the fuselage, such as the typical multiple ejection rack with six 750lb M117 bombs used in Vietnam, although the ground clearance with this load was a mere 7.5in. Tires were inflated to 205psi (140psi for the nose-gear tire) and the three landing gear members were operated by the utility hydraulic system. The wheels had hydraulic brakes with antiskid units fitted after the first F-105B examples.

An arresting hook stressed to 49,000lbs was installed in all aircraft for use in emergency landings, allowing the aircraft to engage arresting gear such as the BAK-9 system at speeds between 120 and 156kts depending on aircraft weight. A 20ft diameter ring-slot braking parachute was housed in a fuselage compartment at the base of the rudder and normally released after touchdown. Its position directly above the afterburner occasionally caused it to emerge as a slightly charred lump rather than a blossoming 'chute if the afterburner had been heavily used. If the parachute was released above the 200kts limiting speed, a frangible pin cut it free to avoid aircraft damage.

Flight Controls

Conventional ailerons were incorporated in the wing but only for subsonic speeds, when they worked in conjunction with five powered spoilers above each wing. At higher speeds, only the spoilers were used for roll control. They were operated by hydraulic actuators, linked to the pilot's control column by push-pull rods and cables. An artificial feel device to simulate the effects of airflow on the control surfaces at different speeds was also linked to the pilot's control column. The wings had Fowler trailing-edge flaps that could be lowered to 34.5 degrees and full-span leading-edge flaps (drooping up to 20 degrees) for takeoff and landing, but also to add lift when the aircraft was maneuvering. The trailing-edge flaps could also be used individually to provide roll control if the vertical tailplane was damaged. It was possible to control an F-105D with a full fuel load including two external wing tanks at speeds between 200–275kts with one flap 100 percent "down" and the other fully up.

The tail surfaces were made of aluminum and magnesium with a steel beam as backbone for the one-piece, all-moving stabilator, operated by

The 4th TFW also introduced the F-105D to USAF service, performing Category II tests of its cockpit displays and avionics in 1961 at Eglin AFB. This F-105D-5-RE (59-1719) is seen during the tests with partial 335th TFS colors. The under-wing markings are placed inboard to clear the pylons and stores. (Republic Aviation)

push-pull rods and dual cables. The vertical stabilizer included a hydraulic rudder. An automatic flight control system (AFCS) provided stability augmentation to each flying control, relaxing the load on the pilot to some extent by "smoothing" the aircraft's flight and reducing the number of control inputs he needed to make.

Hydraulic power came from three separate systems. The first was a utility system to provide for the aircraft's nose-wheel steering, landing gear, brakes and speed brakes, flaps, air intake control, and the drive mechanism for the M61 gun. Two other parallel systems, primary 1 and primary 2, each controlled the spoilers, ailerons, stabilator, and rudder for the left and right sides of the aircraft respectively. Each system had its own hydraulic reservoir, engine-driven pump, and fluid lines running at a maximum pressure of 3000psi. If the J75 engine failed, an emergency ram-air turbine (RAT) could be extended for limited flight control via the primary 1 system. Designers provided no flak-damage protection for the hydraulics, as this wasn't thought necessary for the aircraft's original nuclear strike mission. In combat, however, the hydraulic lines, running close to each other in the aircraft's belly, were frequently damaged by enemy projectiles and the systems rapidly ran down, making the F-105 uncontrollable. Many aircraft were lost when the damaged systems forced the tailplane into a position that caused a steep dive as the pressure dropped. From 1967 most F-105s were retrofitted with a lock, operated by the pilot's "Emerg. Stab." switch, which fixed the stabilator in the neutral position and transferred control authority to emergency pitch and roll switches and the trailing edge flaps. This helped some aircraft to stay aloft a little longer so that the pilots could reach a safer bale-out area. A later, better modification added a further hydraulic reservoir and a set of hydraulic lines in an extra fairing in the fuselage spine, which, powered by the RAT, gave limited use of the stabilator and rudder and also extended the landing gear.

The F-105D and F-105F front cockpits were very similar, with a radar scope at the base of the main panel, the horizontal situation indicator and attitude direction indicator above that, and the two tape displays to each side of them showing airspeed and vertical attitude velocity. (Gary Chambers)

Cockpit

The comparatively spacious, heated cockpit was air-conditioned by a Hamilton Standard system that drew bleed air from the engine. Oxygen came from a 10-litre (2.64 US gallon) supply in the nose, adequate for both single and two-seat F-105 versions. After early design studies for a bulky, box-like structure that would have extended to enclose the pilot for a safe supersonic ejection, Republic elected to use its catapult seat with armor-plated headrest and electrical height adjustment. It included a Koch fiberglass box containing a comprehensive survival kit and one-man raft, and was topped with an MC-1 rubber seat cushion. The pilot's "force-deployed" parachute was worn

Technicians install a J75-P-19W engine in an F-105D, a strenuous task in the heat and humidity of Thailand despite the specially designed hydraulic Model 4000A and 3000E trailers. This task usually had to be repeated at around 125–150 hrs of flying time where engines were routinely pushed to their maximum performance. The rear fuselage was attached with four tension fittings. (Republic Aviation)

separately on his back and formed a back-cushion on the seat. Normally, the parachute opening was delayed in an ejection above 15,500ft so that the pilot could fall into more oxygen-rich atmosphere. At lower altitudes, a zero-delay lanyard was attached, opening the parachute immediately after the pilot separated from his seat. Hinged drag plates extended at each side of the headrest to assist separation. Ejection was initiated by pulling up on the two yellow handles on either side of the seat base. This tightened the pilot's harness and leg restraints, preventing his legs from flailing around during ejection. A further squeeze of a trigger set into the handles jettisoned the canopy, and after 0.3 seconds the seat fired. In two-seat versions ejection could be initiated from either cockpit, but the rear cockpit had to eject first.

The engine throttle was on a console to the pilot's left, which also housed the radar, command radio, fuel and water system, and AFCS controls. The afterburner was engaged by moving the throttle to the left while the engine was running at 80 percent power or more. The pilot could then vary the afterburner within a range from minimum to maximum. The speed brakes were automatically opened 9 degrees to the afterburner position and fuel was directed to the afterburner, which lit between 5 and 8 seconds later, depending on altitude. A similar console on the right held various jettison buttons, the cartridge start button, controls for lights, TACAN (tactical air navigation), Bullpup missiles, the compass, and instrument landing system.

The front panels' main features were the two tape displays, the airspeed/Mach indicator (AMI) to the left of a central attitude director indicator display, and the altitude vertical velocity indicator (AVVI) to the right of it. This "T"-shaped main instrument display presented key information in an easily absorbed way, reducing the pilot's workload. The "special weapons" panel was at the base of this section, and among many other controls and dials were the conventional weapons controls, landing gear, arresting hook and drag 'chute handles, and the radar scope. As Col Ben Fuller recalled, the F-105B cockpit "was very similar to the F-100 Super Sabre. It had round gauges and no ground mapping radar. Later models upgraded to a tape instrument presentation and the very reliable ground map, pencil-beam radar."

The four basic integrated items and displays for the F-105D pilot to use were the ground-mapping and terrain-following radar, the Doppler and navigational computer, the bombing computer (which worked together to navigate and to locate the target), and the autopilot. Pilots could select a 90-degree sector scan on the radar, varying the range from 12 to 80 miles, with the terrain-following mode as the intended choice for low-altitude attack sorties. The Doppler system operated by projecting four radar pencil-beams below the aircraft and measuring the small differences between them, thereby calculating ground speed and the angle between the aircraft's direction and its track across the ground. This information was fed to the navigation computer, enabling it to update the aircraft's latitude/longitude position and to provide distance and bearing to particular destinations or navigational waypoints. It could be updated using the radar or manually from visual cues. The bombing computer was intended for both nuclear "toss" and conventional bombing, but pilots tended to use the manually depressed "pipper" sight rather than the computer.

Although the F-105 was the most sophisticated fighter of its time, pilots generally found the cockpit comfortable, logically planned, and quite easy to operate. They welcomed the aircraft's stability, lack of handling pitfalls, and stellar performance at low altitude.

Engine

Pratt & Whitney's J75-P-19W was rated at 16,100lbs thrust at sea level on a bench test, increasing to 24,500lbs in afterburner and 26,500lbs for a one-minute takeoff boost using the water injection system. This extra power was almost always required for heavyweight combat takeoffs in the hot, humid conditions in Thailand during the Vietnam War. A switch near the throttle triggered the system, spraying water at 110psi into the airflow ahead of the first compressor stage. The water was automatically dumped if injection wasn't used, since the 36-gallon water tank wasn't stressed for in-flight loads and might distort, jamming the rudder cables. The massive powerplant used an eight-stage low-pressure compressor, a seven-stage high-pressure compressor, an eight-stage can annular combustion chamber, a split three-stage turbine, and an afterburner with a two-position nozzle. It was started by a cartridge-pneumatic system, with a connection for external compressed air supply as an alternative.

Fuel system

Internal fuel capacity for the F-105D/F was 1,160 gallons in three bladder tanks in the fuselage. In order to accommodate as much fuel as possible for the big J75, the aft tank was wrapped around the upper part of the engine. Turbine damage or failure could easily drive hot engine debris into this vulnerable tank, causing fires. The internal weapons bay could house a 390-gallon non-jettisonable tank, and an external tank holding either 450 or 650 gallons could be hung on the fuselage centerline pylon. Two 450-gallon tanks with integral pylons could also be fitted to the inboard wing stores attachment points, giving an absolute maximum fuel load of 3,100 gallons, weighing 20,150lbs. In-flight refueling was conducted on early F-105s via a probe which extended from a housing in the nose and engaged a trailing drogue from the tanker aircraft. When the USAF adopted the flying boom in-flight refueling method, a refueling receptacle was added in the upper nose area, and this was retrofitted

The dual options of probe or receptacle in-flight refueling allowed F-105D/Fs to use either drogue or flying boom tankers. Fuel from either input was automatically distributed to all internal and external tanks, which automatically shut off the flow via float-operated switches when full. The flying boom engaged in the receptacle (foreground) with roller latches, and disconnection could be initiated from either tanker or F-105. A last resort "brute force" disconnection option required 4,800lbs of force. (Republic Aviation)

to earlier F-105s. A hydraulic drop-down door opened to reveal a slipway for the tanker's extending refueling boom to make contact with the receptacle. In both cases, fairly subtle aircraft handling was required to achieve a successful link-up without damage to either aircraft. In rough atmospheric conditions, with a heavily loaded fighter, this was always considered a challenge.

Armament

Internal

All production models had a General Electric M61A1 Vulcan 20mm cannon, originally designated T-171E-3. It had six barrels firing 20mm M50 ammunition at a muzzle velocity of 3,380ft per second. The hydraulically driven unit weighed 275lbs and its ammunition supply allowed 10 seconds firing time in bursts of up to 2.5 seconds, with a recommended 1-minute cooling pause between bursts. Pilots in hot pursuit of a MiG found this restriction difficult. In the F-105B the cannon port was just behind the fire-control radome, and the gun was fed via two ammunition chutes. Links and shell cases were returned to storage boxes in the nose in order to maintain the aircraft's trim, as a full ammunition load of around 1,028 rounds weighed almost twice as much as the gun. When the addition of the ASG-19 Thunderstick fire-control system to the F-105D/F necessitated moving the gun further back in the nose, a new feed system was installed using link-less rounds in a large cylindrical drum to which empty shell cases were returned after firing. The entire drum was winched out of the aircraft for reloading.

A centerline multiple ejection rack (MER) with three M117 750lb Tritonal-filled bombs. A standard load was six bombs, but the huge demand for ordnance, particularly for B-52 Arc Light missions, caused shortages between 1965 and 1967. Dense fumes from the Thiokol engine starter cartridge belch from beneath the rear fuselage as another combat sortie begins. (USAF)

Ordnance

Nuclear "special weapons" for the internal bay included one Mk 28 or Mk 43 and a Mk 61 or Mk 57 on each inboard wing pylon or centerline pylon as alternatives. Conventional ordnance covered most options from the TAC arsenal, carried on five ordnance stations and comprising this typical range:

 F-105 Munitions

1. B28 RE nuclear weapon
2. B43-1 nuclear weapon
3. B61 nuclear weapon
4. General Dynamics AGM-78A Standard anti-radiation missile
5. Texas Instruments AGM-45A Shrike anti-radiation missile
6. Ford Aerospace/Raytheon AIM-9B Sidewinder air-to-air missile
7. General Electric M61A1 Vulcan 20mm rotary cannon
8. SUU-30A with CBU-24 munitions
9. SUU-30HB with CBU-71 munitions
10. M117 820lb bomb
11. Mk84 1,972lb low-drag general purpose bomb
12. Mk 82SE 570lb Snakeye bomb
13. Mk 82 520lb low-drag general purpose bomb with fuse extender
14. Mk 81 260lb low-drag general purpose bomb with 36in. fuse extender

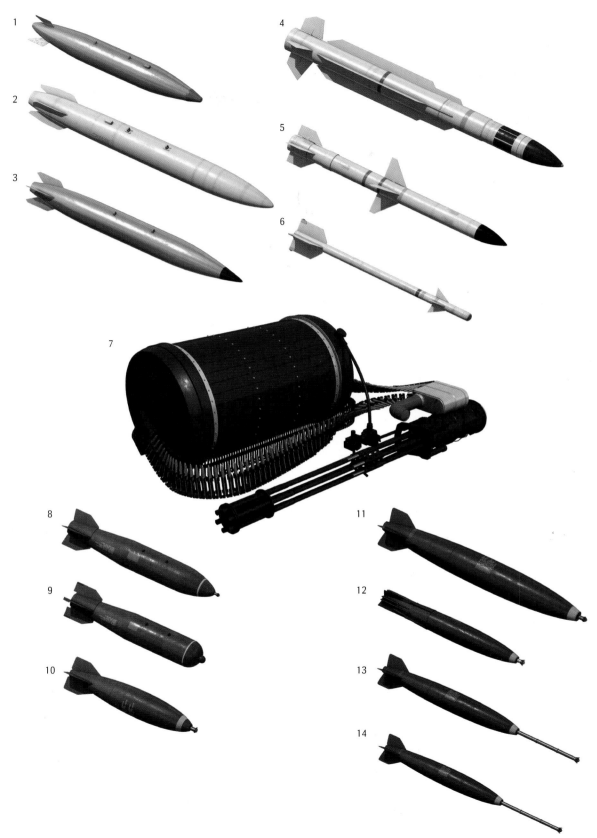

Using a special rig attached to an MJ-1 weapons loader, Takhli armament technicians load an ammunition drum into 354th TFS F-105D-31-RE 62-4387 in 1969. Although the drum could hold 1,130 rounds, the usual complement was 1,028, enough for 10 seconds' firing time. (USAF)

Centerline pylon – a multiple ejection rack (MER) with either:
6x M117 806lb bombs (retarded or destructor), or 6x Mk 82 510lb bombs (with Mk 82 "Snakeye" alternatives)
3x Mk 83 1,000lb bombs or one Mk 84 2,020lb bomb or one M118 3,000lb bomb
6x M129 leaflet bombs, MC-1 chemical bombs or MLU-32 flares
5x SUU-30 with CBU-24, -29, -49, -53 or -64 cluster bomblets
3x BLU-1/B or 2x BLU-27 fire bombs (napalm), or 3x BLU-31 mines
An SUU-21 practice bomb dispenser
Inboard wing pylons (2) – each could carry either:
4x Mk 82/Mk 82 "Snakeye" or M117 on a MER, or 2x Mk 83 or one Mk 84 bomb.
4x SUU-30 CBU dispensers (CBU-24, 29, 49, 53, 54)
2x BLU-27 or BLU-1/B fire bombs, 2x BLU-52 or 4x MC- chemical bombs, M129 dispensers or BLU-31 mines
2x LAU-32 or LAU-52 seven-shot rocket launchers or 2x LAU-3/A or LAU-18/A 19-shot rocket launchers
1x AGM-12B/C Bullpup air-to-ground missile (with pylon adapter)
The F-105G could also carry the AGM-78 Standard ARM antiradiation missile on a pylon adapter.
Outboard wing pylons (2) – each could carry either:
1x Mk 82, Mk 83 or M117 bomb
1x BLU-27 or BLU-1/B fire bomb
1x BLU-52 chemical bomb or 1x SUU-10 (CBU-3) or SUU-30 (CBU-24,-29, -49, -53, -54) dispenser or M129 leaflet bomb
1x AIM-9B or AIM-9E Sidewinder air-to-air missile (or two on a dual launcher, tested on a JF-105B and used on some F-105Ds in Vietnam)
1x LAU-3 2.75in rocket pod
1x AGM-12B/C Bullpup air-to-ground missile or AGM-45A Shrike antiradiation missile (not for F-105B), with pylon adapters in both cases

A 355th TFW F-105D-31-RE (62-4297) in 1964, showing off its internal cannon, under-wing AGM-12 Bullpup B missile ,and 2.75in. rocket pod. The centerline MER has six M117s. Two nuclear weapons, a Mk 61 (left) and Mk 28 (right), are on stands beside the aircraft. The former was carried on an inboard or centerline pylon. (Author's collection)

Dimensions

F-105 variant	Wingspan	Length*	Height	Wing area	Tailplane span
F-105A	34ft 9in.	61ft 5in.	17ft 6in.	385sq ft	17ft 3in.
F-105B	34ft 9in.	63ft 1in.	19ft 8in.	385sq ft	17ft 3in.
F-105D	34ft 9in.	64ft 4in.	19ft 8in.	385sq ft	17ft 3in.
F-105F/G 34ft 9in.	67ft 0in.	20ft 5in.	385sq ft	17ft 3in.	F-105F/G 34ft 9in.

*includes horizontal tail surfaces but not pitot boom

Weights (lbs), takeoff run (ft) to clear 50 ft obstacle

F-105 variant	Empty	Combat (basic mission)	Max Takeoff	Landing	Take-off run
YF-105A	21,010	28,966	41,500	–	4,020ft
F-105B	25,855	34,870	46,998	29,576	6,220ft
F-105D	27,500	35,637	52,838	32,393	5,830ft
F-105F	30,419	38,738	54,580	33,800	7,770ft
F-105G	31,279	41,091	54,590	35,266	8,210ft

Performance*

F-105 variant	Max (sea level/36,000ft/ stalling)	Combat cruise	Combat ceiling	Combat radius	Ferry range
YF-105A	778/857/ 185	500	49,950	–	1010
F-105B	864/1,195/177	508	32,750	646	1935
F-105D	726/1,192/180	501	28,200	676	1917
F-105F	681/723/186	502	26,800	459	1300
F-105G	681/723/188	504	24,600	391	1,623

*speed (mph), altitude (ft), range (miles)

N.B. These figures were recorded under test conditions with typical takeoff weights, and they would be significantly degraded by high ambient temperatures, humidity, and aircraft wear.

Main production

F-105 variant	Block numbers	Serials	Number built	First flight
YF-105A	-1-RE	54-0098 to 54-0099	2	October 22, 1955
F-105B	-1-RE to -20-RE	54-0100 to 57-5840	75	May 26, 1956
JF-105B	-1-RE to -2-RE	54-0105, -0108, -0111	3	July 18, 1957
F-105D	-1-RE to -31-RE	58-1146 to 62-4411	610	June 9, 1959
F-105F	-1-RE	62-4412 to 63-8366	143	June 11, 1963

AIM-9B Sidewinders ready to upload. The "ZA" coded 12th TFS F-105D with a twin AIM-9 launcher is seen in 1968, when the squadron deployed to Osan AB, South Korea for Operation *Coronet Wasp* in response to the North Korean seizure of the intelligence-gathering ship USS *Pueblo*. (USAF)

F-105 CONVERSIONS, MODIFICATIONS AND PROJECTS

Project Look-Alike

In order to bring all its operational F-105Bs up to the same standard of wiring, hydraulic, and flying control equipment, the USAF grounded the fleet (after two major accidents) and modified all aircraft by November 1962 under Project Big Bear. This extended to the F-105D fleet, which had been manufactured with some variation in standard, depending on block number. Early aircraft had catapult rather than rocket ejection seats, and lacked "blind toss" bombing or the ability to launch the AGM-12 Bullpup, carry the 650-gallon centerline fuel tank or refuel in flight, except with the probe-and-drogue method.

Bullpup B was designed to a US Navy requirement for a Mach 1.75 standoff missile using a 250lb bomb as its warhead in a 13.5ft body weighing 1785lbs and powered by a liquid-propellant rocket. Steering was accomplished by radio signals, with a small "joystick" control added to the F-105 cockpit. The pilot sighted the missile after launching it in a 20-degree dive by watching tracking flares attached to its tailfins, but he had to follow in the missile's path to guide it until it impacted. The weapon's limited destructive power and the unwelcome requirement for the F-105 pilot to maintain a straight course directly towards enemy defenses for each missile launched reduced its operational use after the opening stages of the Vietnam War.

Project Look-Alike brought all F-105Ds up to the equipment standard of the final Block 31 production, including provision for "flying boom" refueling via a receptacle ahead of the windscreen. Although the latter modification brought some discomfort to pilots, as fuel often sprayed back over the cockpit air intake area, causing stinging fumes, it enabled the F-105 to be refueled by the main USAF tanker fleet – a crucial factor for wartime operations. The rework program also included the painting of all F-105B/Ds with a clear lacquer that included 12oz of aluminum paste per gallon. Serious corrosion had been found in F-105Bs, and it occurred too in F-105Ds based in the damp conditions of central Europe. The lacquer finish helped to water-seal the various seams and joins in the skin.

Thunderbird F-105B

Nine F-105Bs were modified for use by the 4520th Air Demonstration Squadron (the Thunderbirds) when it was decided in May 1963 to replace the team's F-100C Super Sabres. Tests were conducted on several F-105Bs to assess the type's suitability, and nine aircraft from the 4th TFW were modified and delivered between December 1963 and April 1964. Republic Aviation replaced the M61 cannon and ammunition supply together with the MA-8 fire-control system with ballast and two 50-gallon tanks to hold smoke-creating light oil. The bomb bay was converted into a baggage compartment and the flight controls were upgraded to F-105D specification. Afterburner light-up time was reduced to 2 seconds from the usual 4–5 seconds and flaps were modified so that they could be lowered 4 degrees at speeds above 500kts. Four aircraft had new stainless steel vertical tails to withstand the exhaust efflux when flying in the "slot" position to another F-105B and the extra stress involved in the team's "knife" maneuver.

Six shows were flown in the 1964 season, but Capt Gene Devlin was killed when his aircraft (57-5801) suffered a major structural failure of a splice-plate on the upper fuselage. It broke in half ahead of the bomb bay as he made a high-G pullup from formation to land at Hamilton AFB in California. All F-105Bs were subsequently given reinforced splice-plates in Project Backbone. The accident caused all F-105s to be grounded, and the USAF decided to revert to the F-100D Super Sabre for the rest of the season, keeping to that type when it was clear that further modifications to the F-105Bs would be impractical. The surviving Thunderbird F-105Bs had their operational equipment reinstalled and they were reassigned to the 141st TFS, New Jersey Air National Guard by the end of 1966.

Thunderbird F-105B serials: 57-5782/87/90/93/97/98, -5801/02/14.

RF-105B (AP-71)/JF-105B

Three aircraft from the first production of F-105Bs were initially ordered as RF-105Bs, the remainder of the January 19, 1955 order for 55 F-105Bs and 17 RF-105B reconnaissance fighters. Other developments with advanced all-weather and night-reconnaissance systems were studied, but abandoned as the necessary equipment was still at a very early stage of development. These first three aircraft were built to take a KS-24A oblique and vertical camera system in place of the M61 gun, which was replaced by two M39 20mm guns in blister fairings on the fuselage. An oblique TV camera was mounted in the nose with a monitor TV screen in the cockpit. RF-105Bs were planned for TAC reconnaissance wings at Shaw AFB, South Carolina, Spangdahlem AB, Germany and Kadena AB, Okinawa. Work on the project was terminated on January 14, 1957 and the McDonnell RF-101C Voodoo was chosen for the mission instead. The three RF-105Bs were redesignated JF-105B to indicate temporary special test status and used by Republic for a series of tests including ordnance separation and high-speed control "flutter," with test equipment installed in the capacious camera bay.

JF-105B serials: 54-0105, -0108, -0112.

The raised spine on F-105D-10-RE 60-0475 houses its Thunderstick II avionics. This was the sixth aircraft to be modified. The "TH"-coded 457th TFS, AFRES operated T-Stick II aircraft and F-105Fs from 1972 to 1981. (Author's collection)

F-105C (AP-63-5) and F-105E

Adding a two-seat training version to the production run of any Century Series fighter was standard, and in May 1956 the USAF's Air Training Command ordered five two-seat F-105Cs (54-0113 to -0117), added to the order for 82 F-105B/RF-105Bs. The redesign retained the basic F-105B but added a single, rearward-hinged bubble canopy to cover the second, tandem cockpit. The full F-105B systems were included, butinternal fuel tankage was reduced by 155 gallons. A mockup was produced in November 1956 and the USAF contract situation fluctuated between 5 and 45 aircraft before final cancellation in October 1957 in favor of a two-seat F-105D variant, the F-105E (AP-63-33). Plans called for 89 F-105Es in May 1958, but budget restrictions caused their cancellation as well in April 1959 in favor of the same number of cheaper F-105Ds. The F-105E would have had the same overall dimensions and equipment as the F-105D, with a one-piece transparency over the two cockpits, and the same fuel reduction as for the F-105C. Cost-saving by the USAF again caused cancellation of the 26 aircraft ordered in November 1958, and the eight F-105Es already on the assembly lines were converted into F-105D-6-REs (serial numbers 59-1817 to -1826).

F-105D Thunderstick II

The main production version of the F-105 received its only major update in 1969 in response to operational experience in Vietnam. In combat, the ASG-19 fire-control system had revealed limited accuracy with conventional weapons, particularly at night and in poor weather. The advent of solid-state electronics enabled a major update to the R-14 radar to R-14A standard. An ITT AN/ARN-92 LORAN receiver and a gyro-compass attitude vertical reference system worked with the Doppler navigation unit and radar to give greater bombing accuracy and effective terrain avoidance for low-altitude flight. The new equipment was housed in a long fairing above the fuselage. Thirty aircraft were selected for conversion between May 1970 and July 1971, although they were too late to participate in the Vietnam War as the F-105D had already been withdrawn from the conflict. They flew with the 23rd TFW in 1971, then moved to Air Force Reserve service with the 457th TFS at Carswell AFB, Texas.

T-Stick II serials: 60-0455, -0458,-0464/5, -0471, -0475, -0480, -0490, -0493, -0500, -0513, -0517, -0521, -0527/8, -0533, -5375/6, 61-0044, -0047, -0063/4, -0074/5/6, -0080, -0096, -0100, -0110, -0161.

RF-105D

Republic continued to pursue reconnaissance versions of the F-105, and an amendment to the basic USAF requirement for the Thunderchief (GOR-49) specified a version with cameras, sideways-looking radar in a pod, in-flight film processing, and various electronic intelligence-gathering devices. The company received instructions to develop this version on June 2, 1961 with the prospect of building more than 100 aircraft, but the project was canceled at the end of that year and many of the proposed RF-105D systems eventually appeared instead in the McDonnell RF-4C Phantom II two years later.

F-105F

The requirement for a two-seat Thunderchief for proficiency and radar navigation training was finally met in May 1962 when authorization for the F-105F was given by Secretary of Defense Robert McNamara. It differed considerably from the proposed F-105E in having an extended fuselage. A 31in. section was added just forward of the wing and two electronics compartments were repositioned. To maintain the center of gravity and improve stability, the vertical tail was increased in height by 5in. and 15 percent was added to its area. The consequent 3,000lbs extra weight, including reinforcement of the rear fuselage, meant beefing up the undercarriage. Two separate cockpit canopies were fitted, opening to a 75-degree angle rather than the 42 degrees of the F-105B/D. As well as offering training functions, the aircraft was intended to be as fully combat-capable as the F-105D. Missions could be flown without the rear cockpit occupant. This happened in Vietnam, where F-105Fs were quite often flown as single-pilot aircraft in flights of F-105Ds. The first F-105F (62-4412) flew at Mach 1.15 on its June 11, 1963 maiden flight, and production examples were delivered from December 7, 1963. The F-105F contract allowed for an initial 36 aircraft followed by 107 more, although this larger batch had to replace the last 143 F-105Ds, reducing the overall cost of the F-105F purchase by $8m. The final Thunderchief, F-105F 63-8366, left the Farmingdale factory in December 1964.

F-105F conversions

Combat Martin
Ten F-105Fs were modified in 1967 to carry the Hallicrafters QRC-128 (AN/ALQ-59) communications-jamming equipment as a means of disrupting North Vietnamese ground control of their MiG fighters. The equipment was also fitted to EB-66 jamming aircraft. Installation in the F-105F involved removal of the rear seat and most of the instrument panel to accommodate "Colonel Computer" – the ALQ-59. The other distinctive visual feature was a large blade antenna behind the rear canopy. Although the Combat Martin F-105Fs flew many missions over Vietnam as single-seat bombers, their pilots apparently never received authorization to use the ALQ-59 in its intended role, and the eight surviving aircraft were eventually converted into F-105Gs.

Combat Martin serials: 62-4432, -4435, -4443/4, 63-8268, -8280, -8291, -8318, -8336/7.

Project Northscope/Commando Nail
The F-105D's bombing accuracy was challenged by the monsoon conditions of Southeast Asia, and the USAF realized that the US Navy had a much more effective night/all-weather attack aircraft in its A-6A Intruder. This subsonic

A trio of F-105F Ryan's Raiders with the TCTO 1F-105F-536 blind bombing modification. Prior to its more specialized uses, the F-105F was employed, as Ben Fuller recalled, for aircrew tactical proficiency assessments and "the annual instrument check ride. There were only a couple of F-105Fs in each squadron so they were only used for instrument training and check rides, as well as theatre indoctrination." (Jerry Arruda via Norm Taylor)

bomber could penetrate enemy defenses on solo, low-altitude attack missions in ways that would be matched after 1968 by the Air Force's General Dynamics F-111A. Until then, the USAF's F-105s were effectively grounded by weather or diverted to Combat Skyspot targets. As an interim measure General John Ryan, Commander of Pacific Air Forces, initiated a training scheme for 25 selected F-105 pilots, many of them instructors, who became known as Ryan's Raiders in their parent unit, the 388th TFW. The aim was to use the ASG-19 and R-14A radar as effectively as possible in all-weather attacks on North Vietnam. Systems were tweaked as part of the Project Northscope "blind bombing modification" (TO 1F-105F-536) that replaced the control column, nuclear panel, and radar scope in the rear cockpit with a larger 5in. scope and an ER-142 panoramic receiver to detect enemy radar sites. The undersides of the aircraft were camouflaged for low-altitude Commando Nail night operations, which began on April 26, 1967 and continued, despite six losses, until November 1968. Generally, the F-105F's accuracy was still only half that of the A-6A.

Twenty F-105Fs received "blind bombing" modifications: 62-4419, -4424, -4428/9, -4446, -8274, 63-8263, -8269, -8274 to -8278, -8281, -8285, -8293, -8312, -8327, -8346, -8353.

F-105D European

An unsuccessful 1960 Republic proposal for F-105Ds as French and British purchases included the prospect of a license-built J75 in the French version or a 34,200lbs thrust Bristol Olympus B01 22R (the TSR 2's powerplant) for the RAF.

F-105F/G Wild Weasel

This final, heaviest and most complex Thunderchief was the culmination of an intensive program that began in response to the shooting down of a USAF F-4C Phantom II on July 27, 1965 by a North Vietnamese SA-2 SAM. A team led by Brig Gen Kenneth Dempster investigated the threat and recommended that a hunter-killer force of tactical aircraft, equipped with effective electronic countermeasures devices and weapons, should be sent to Southeast Asia to detect and attack the SAM launch sites. The other main recommendation was the provision of QRC-160-1 jamming pods for carriage by strike aircraft in high-threat areas. Fortunately, a California company, Applied Technology

Inc. (ATI), was able to supply its Vector IV radar homing and warning (RHAW) set, IR-133 panoramic receiver, and WR-300 launch warning receiver to equip a SAM detection fighter. The system was tested operationally in F-100F Super Sabres in Vietnam as the Wild Weasel I project.

Republic had already begun to test the Bendix APS-107 RHAW pod in an F-105D in July 1965, but it had limited success and required much development. As an urgent alternative the Vector IV system was installed in F-105D 62-4291 in only five days, while another F-105D (61-0138) tested a rival Bendix/ Maxson system. The USAF ordered 500 Vector IV sets even before testing began, such was the concern over increasing F-105 losses. Encouraged by the success of Wild Weasel I, the USAF had seven F-105Fs equipped with the ATI suite, now in production as the APR-25, APR-26 launch warning set and IR-133 (later replaced by the ER-142) as Wild Weasel III. Unlike the F-100F, the F-105Fs were also able to launch the AGM-45 Shrike antiradiation missile. After initial installation difficulties and the addition of another system (ATI's AE-100 azimuth-elevation set for displaying the location of a threat radar in the pilot's optical sight), the seven aircraft were modified and tested in February to March 1966. Five were sent to Korat RTAFB on May 22, 1966 to begin operational trials.

With two Shrikes and a Standard ARM aboard, an F-105G tops off its fuel tanks before heading for its target. After firing the AGM-78, the single external fuel tank could be retained with some careful control trimming. Two AGM-78s were occasionally loaded, but this limited the fuel to internal and belly-tank and required a significantly overweight takeoff. (USAF)

A number of alternative antiradar devices were tested in these and subsequent F-105Fs, including the SEE-SAMS, which gave a specific warning to any aircraft that was directly targeted by a SAM's "Fan Song" guidance radar.

Despite initial losses on their hazardous missions, the Wild Weasel III crews proved the concept sufficiently for the USAF to order a total of 86 conversions to destroy and suppress SA-2 radars and protect the F-105 strike forces as hunter-killer flights with F-105D bombers. A further development was the move to equip Wild Weasel F-105Fs with self-protection jamming. This didn't require external pods using pylons that could carry fuel or Shrikes. The solution was a pair of external blister fairings on the lower central fuselage, housing a QRC-380 (later ALQ-105) system with QRC-335 jammer devices. Essentially, it was a pylon-mounted ALQ-101 ECM pod divided between the two "scabbed" fairings.

To improve the Wild Weasels' hitting power, General Dynamics produced the AGM-78A Mod 0 antiradiation missile in 1967, and it entered service with the 355th TFW's F-105F Weasels in February 1968. However, the termination of bombing north of the 19th parallel on April 1, 1968 halted its combat use by USAF aircraft until 1971. Later in 1968 modification work began to incorporate the improved AGM-78B Mod 1. At the same time, Weasel F-105Fs were reequipped with improved APR-36 and APR-37 sets, replacing the APR-25 and APR-26. A better panoramic scanner, the APR-35, replaced the ER-142 version, and the electronic warfare officer's (EWO's) panels were redesigned. The improvements were sufficient to warrant a redesignation as the F-105G from October 1969. Funds were made available to update all surviving Weasel F-105Fs to this standard, and 65 aircraft eventually became F-105G-1-REs.

Wild Weasel weapons

The Texas Instruments AGM-45A Shrike was the first tactical antiradiation missile in the US armory, entering service in 1963 after development under US Navy contracts. Its passive seeker head, which came in a dozen types for different radar targets, had to be tuned to a specific type of radar emission before the carrier F-105 took off. The enemy radar operator's best defense was to "switch off" if a Shrike launch was detected via small metallic particles in its rocket exhaust. Lacking any memory of the target's location, the Shrike then entered a ballistic trajectory, probably missing its target. It could only be launched when the F-105 crew had already detected an enemy radar and pointed the missile towards its estimated location. Four missiles could be carried on double launchers, though the usual load was two for F-105F/Gs and some F-105Ds. Its effective range was typically 6 miles when launched from the Weasel's usual operational altitudes, which placed the launch aircraft well within the SA-2's 18-mile lethal range. It could be "lofted" from a slight climb to increase range to 12–14 miles. The missile's 145lb warhead could destroy a "Fan Song" radar scanner in a direct hit, but it was too small to inflict more serious damage on the radar site, and hits were hard to detect from the air except by timing when radars ceased transmissions following a Shrike launch.

AGM-45A Shrike	
Length	9ft
Diameter	8in.
Span	36in.
Weight	390lbs
Power	Rocketdyne Mk 39 or Aerojet Mk 53 solid-propellant rocket motor
Speed	Mach 2
Fusing	Impact and proximity types

The General Dynamics AGM-78A Standard ARM was another US Navy-sponsored design based on the ship-borne RIM-66 Standard surface-to-air missile, and entered naval service in 1968 with a similar passive seeker to the Shrike. In its AGM-78B version, a new gimballed seeker with in-built memory was used. This required no pre-launch tuning and could store the coordinates of a radar emitter even after it had switched off, thus maintaining its attack course. Much larger than the Shrike, the AGM-78 was slung beneath a special General Dynamics LAU-80 pylon on an inboard wing station. Due to the cost, drag, and relative scarcity of AGM-78s, only one was usually loaded, with

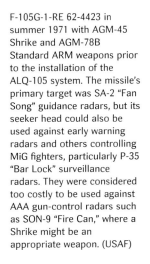

F-105G-1-RE 62-4423 in summer 1971 with AGM-45 Shrike and AGM-78B Standard ARM weapons prior to the installation of the ALQ-105 system. The missile's primary target was SA-2 "Fan Song" guidance radars, but its seeker head could also be used against early warning radars and others controlling MiG fighters, particularly P-35 "Bar Lock" surveillance radars. They were considered too costly to be used against AAA gun-control radars such as SON-9 "Fire Can," where a Shrike might be an appropriate weapon. (USAF)

a 450-gallon tank on the opposite pylon providing equilibrium. The missile could be launched "off axis," meaning that the F-105G need not be flying directly towards the target at the point of launch.

Standard ARM	
Length	15ft
Diameter	13.5in.
Span	43in.
Weight	1,356lbs, including warhead of 215lbs
Power	Aerojet Mk 27 solid-propellant rocket
Speed	Mach 2.5
Maximum range	58 miles

OPERATIONAL HISTORY

The F-105's operational introduction was slowed by continuing development and production problems in 1959, but the first USAF Thunderchief wing, the 4th TFW, had received 60 F-105Bs by January 1960, and it was operationally ready from April 1961. The 335th TFS tested F-105Ds from December 1960, but the wing's F-105Bs were not fully replaced by F-105Ds until early 1964. It was with this mixture of F-105s that the 4th TFW faced the Thunderchief's first potential combat situation on October 18, 1962, in response to the discovery of Russian SS-4 "Sandal" ballistic missile emplacements in Cuba. The 334th, 335th, and 336th TFS, reinforced by 20 F-105s from the 4520th CCTW at Nellis AFB, were sent to McCoy AFB, Florida, ready to strike the missile sites.

Col Ben Fuller was among those pilots.

> We were told it was top secret and we weren't to tell our wives and relatives where we were going – a night deployment to McCoy AFB, Florida, which was very dangerous due to so many planes trying to land there at the same time in night VFR [visual flight rules] conditions. We spent one or two days getting familiar with the SAC alert facility that would become our operations center and then returned to home base [Seymour Johnson AFB]. Several days later we were alerted again and deployed some 65 F-105B/Ds back to McCoy – this time in daylight, and not so hairy. This probably coincided with the DEFCON 3 [defense readiness condition] of October 22. The Cuban Missile Crisis had begun to get hot.

A bare-metal-finished F-105D-10-RE (60-0438) of the 22nd TFS over Germany in 1961. This was the first 36th TFW squadron to convert to the F-105D when its pilots began training with the 4520th CCTW in March 1961 and began ferrying their new aircraft to Bitburg AB in May. The aircraft was officially accepted into USAFE service at the June 1961 Paris Air Show. (via Norm Taylor)

This 7th TFS, 49th TFW F-105D is about to be started by its pilot, 1st Lt Carter, for a sortie as part of the 4th AIRCENT Tactical Weapons Meet at Chaumont AB, France. Spangdahlem's first F-105D arrived on October 30, 1961 and reequipment was complete by mid-1962. (USAF)

President Kennedy announced the naval "quarantine" blockade of Cuba and the evacuation of the US Navy base at Guantanamo Bay on October 22. Col Fuller recalled that they had been assigned targets before redeploying to McCoy.

I was in a flight led by Capt Sandy Vandenberg, son of General Hoyt Vandenberg [USAF Chief of Staff 1948–53]. Sandy was chosen to brief General Curtis LeMay on our flight plan and target, which was Santa Clara airbase in eastern Cuba and he had prepared well for this important guest. [

LeMay opposed the blockade, favoring bombing of the missile sites and occupation of Cuba.

Sandy began with a paper-covered easel and as he said, "General LeMay, this is the most current picture we have of our target," he flipped the paper and showed a large

picture of the airbase that had appeared in the *Miami Herald* newspaper! That finished the briefing, and from then on all aerial reconnaissance pictures were sent to the operational bases before going to Washington.

For the two weeks at McCoy we spent the days on 15-minute alert. We would assume alert 30 minutes before sunrise at the target and go off alert at sunset: it would have been a VFR war for the F-105s. I am not sure we would have been too successful on our strike since many of the F-105s were loaded with napalm, which would have worked against "soft" targets like aircraft but not "hard" targets at Santa Clara. There was also something about how long a batch of napalm was good for after being mixed; our planes were on alert for many days. We did have a few practice scrambles, and it was something to behold. My F-105 was parked between the dual runways, and it was a wild drive taking the crews to their steeds. With all those planes starting up with gunpowder cartridges, it looked like the force was on fire!

The Cuba crisis faded, but the 4th TFW was to experience a real war soon enough in Southeast Asia. Before that, the 334th TFS made the F-105's first NATO deployment, sending 18 F-105Bs to Moron AB, Spain, in April 1963. After conversion to the F-105D in 1964, it operated out of Incirlik AB, Turkey, on a May 1965 NATO support deployment. As Ben Fuller recalled, the wing's F-105s also

flew in the fly-by for President Kennedy's funeral in Washington, DC on November, 25, 1963. Along with 20 US Navy planes, the 30 "Thuds" made up one aircraft per state of the USA. Picture a gaggle of 50 fighters trying to maintain some semblance of formation and timing while a horse-drawn caisson clops over to Arlington!

In the Far East several Pacific Air Force (PACAF) nuclear-capable F-100 Super Sabre units began to transition to the F-105. First was the 18th TFW at Kadena AB, Okinawa, which began conversion when three F-105Ds arrived on October 30, 1962 for its 67th TFS. The 44th TFS followed in November 1962 and the 12th TFS at the end of that year. The 8th TFW, tasked with the defense of Japan and South Korea since 1950, became the second PACAF wing to receive F-105Ds for its three squadrons from spring 1963 under Col William E. Buck, although the closure of its Itazuke base the following year caused its reassignment to George AFB, California. A third wing, the 41st Air

PILOT'S PERSONAL FLIGHT EQUIPMENT

The bush hat worn by this 388th TFW pilot will be replaced on entering the aircraft by his helmet (typically an HGU-2AP or later form-fit model) with built-in oxygen mask and microphone. The gray-green nylon vest (Lancer-Clinton Corps. SRU-21/P was common) was worn over the basic flying suit and loaded with weighty survival gear. According to Capt James Walbridge, shot down in a 421st TFS F-105D on February 28, 1967, "Every ounce was worth its weight in gold when you were on the ground [after a shoot-down]." Usually the top pair of pockets held an MC-1 or lensatic compass and extra .38cal bullets and waterproof matches. The next pocket down contained a survival first aid kit, and the two pockets below that had a Mk 3 Type 1, 2in. signal mirror, an M201 signal kit containing a miniature launcher, and seven red flares for the pilot to mark his position for rescuers. There was also marker dye for the same purpose in the frequent case of an ejection over water. The lower pair of pockets would often hold several survival radios (Type 3, RT-10, URC-64, PR-90 and others). Capt Walbridge was not unusual in loading three radios in his vest. Under the pilot's left armpit, but hanging slightly behind his back when seated, was a holster with a Smith and Wesson .38 snub nose sidearm, although some pilots preferred a 9mm pistol. Standard ammunition issue was 17 rounds of ball ammunition and six of tracer, though more were often carried.

Over the waist and legs the pilot wore a G-suit ("speed jeans"), which pressurized under high G, retaining the blood in the upper part of his body to reduce blackouts. There is a clip on the left thigh for holding mission cards and a left leg pocket for a 250ft length of nylon tape to aid descent from high treetops if the ejection was over jungle terrain. The right leg pockets had room for two "baby" bottles for water, a survival knife, and an escape and evasion kit. The parachute was worn on the pilot's back rather than being part of the seat as it was in later ejection seats such as the Martin-Baker Mk 5/7, and it was connected to the seat belts via a bail-out lanyard. It was carried to the aircraft, dumped at the foot of the ladder while the pilot did his pre-flight inspection, and strapped on before climbing into the cockpit. The survival kit was ejected with the pilot and contained a full range of survival gear including radios, flares, mirrors, a whistle – and even a spare pair of socks.

The first batch of F-105D-25-REs for the 18th TFW pauses at Hickam AB, Hawaii on October 23, 1962 before continuing the journey to Kadena AB, Okinawa. By October 1967 three of them had been lost over North Vietnam. 61-0163, "Tommy's Hawk," reportedly went out of control when only one of its 3,000lb bombs released while attacking a bridge target. (USAF)

Division/6441st TFW at Yokota, Japan, took on the three ex-8th TFW squadrons (the 35th, 36th, and 80th TFS) from June 18, 1964. On August 12, 1964 the 36th TFS sent the first F-105Ds into combat in Southeast Asia from Korat RTAFB, Thailand, but the wing's principal duty was round-the-clock nuclear alert at Yokota and Osan, in Korea. By 1966, the increasing wartime demands on other F-105 units that had previously deployed to share the alert burden meant that Yokota pilots were spending half their time at Osan.

Bill Hosmer was one of the 18th TFW pilots at Kadena, rehearsing for Armageddon.

Sitting alert at Kadena with those two Y-1, 1.1 megaton bombs was an ominous situation for me. I was scheduled to strike Shanghai Airport first, then another target. After that I was supposed to head east until flame out, when I would eject and be picked up by a US Navy destroyer. I think there was an assigned heading for the egress route so the ship would be somewhere near where I would end up after the fuel burned out.

Ironically, in the 1980s Bill had to deliver a Cessna Citation business jet to China, via Shanghai Airport. He was able to show the pilot the land feature

The 41st AD took over the 8th TFW's three F-105 units in June 1964 at Yokota AB, Japan for nuclear alert, but it also managed the F-105's combat introduction in August 1964 with rotational TDYs to Korat RTAFB. This 35th TFS F-105F-1-RE (63-8280) is seen near Mount Fuji with F-105D-31-RE 62-4355 of the 80th TFS. (USAF)

on the weather radar that would have marked the starting point (IP) for his approach to the airport target, and weapons delivery.

> I remembered having to draw the predicted radar return when getting certified on my target. It was déjà vu all over again.

In Europe, the same type of nuclear alert role was performed by two F-105 wings in West Germany, the 36th TFW at Bitburg AB and the 49th TFW at Spangdahlem. The Bitburg wing was the first overseas tactical fighter wing to convert to the F-105 when the pilots of its 22nd TFS relinquished their Super Sabres and began training at Nellis AFB in March 1961. All three Bitburg squadrons were combat ready by the end of 1961, having qualified in both nuclear and conventional weapons delivery at the USAFE (US Air Forces Europe) Weapons Center, Wheelus AB, Libya, in keeping with President John F. Kennedy's policy of "flexible response" rather than a pure nuclear deterrent role. Spangdahlem's F-105s were all in place by mid-1962, performing the same role as the 36th TFW Thunderchiefs.

Bob "Spade" Cooley was a captain with the 9th TFS at Spangdahlem, having flown the F-86 Sabre in Korea in 1954, followed by the F-86F Thunderstreak and the F-100 Super Sabre. Compared with the F-100, he found the F-105 handled similarly but

> it had a lot more power. Its mission was essentially the same as the Super Sabre, and I didn't have lot of trouble going from one to the other. There was a constant flow of planes from Bitburg and Spangdahlem to Wheelus. They had to come back to base for maintenance and we just took our turn for nuclear and conventional training on the El Uotia Bombing Range including skip bombing, dive bombing, and gunnery. Each pilot was required to do two weeks every quarter at Wheelus.

If fate had called upon the pilots to carry out a real nuclear mission, they would have relied on the F-105's speed to evade opposing fighters.

> Nothing was as fast as a "Thud" when it got going. It was the world's fastest tricycle. It had no air-to-air role unless forced into it.

Some of the training took place in European airspace. Ben Fuller was also at Spangdahlem, with the 7th TFS.

The 23rd TFW replaced the 388th TFW at McConnell AFB, Kansas in February 1964. Later that year it took part in Exercise *Goldfire 1* at Whiteman AFB, Missouri, developing tactical air support innovations for TAC. F-105F-1-RE 63-83332, decorated here with green bands on its wings and fuselage for the exercise, later returned to the 23rd TFW as an F-105G, flew in combat as "Draggin' Ass," and continued in service until March 1983. (USAF)

Our normal training consisted of flying radar low-level navigation and simulated bombing of targets throughout France and West Germany. The mission profile was low-level to the target and then a climb out to altitude for an instrument approach and landing using GCA [ground-controlled approach] assistance. Due to European weather almost all landings were under instrument conditions. Tactical proficiency check-rides involved a simulated strike against one of the several pre-planned routes that each squadron had on file.

Between 1964 and 1966 at the USAFE F-105 bases, the nuclear weapons on "alert" aircraft were the Mk 43 and Mk 57.

These weapons contained drag parachutes and were primarily designed for low-level or "toss" delivery. For this reason the "over the shoulder" LABS maneuver done by the F-100s wasn't much used. Occasionally, live bombing time would become available at Suippes Range in France, mostly when weather permitted and during operational readiness inspections [ORIs], at which times low-level profiles would be flown with the target being the Suippes Range. The initial arrival at Suippes would be the assigned time on target [TOT] and the first bomb dropped would simulate the nuclear weapon.

Using the nuclear deterrent, with all its terrifying potential, required F-105 pilots to

sit on a 15-minute alert with a live nuclear weapon. The alert facility was at the end of the runway and each aircraft was in a covered bunker, guarded by a member of the air police. Access to the plane was by visual recognition. Each guard personally met the pilot at the beginning of his shift and had a 10x8 photo of him. Most alert tours were three days in length and pilots were on alert 24 hours a day. At least once during his tour, the pilot would start his plane and check out the systems and rotate the tires. For safety, the plane would be blocked by a fire truck so no takeoff could occur. In addition all planes were equipped with the permissive action link [PAL] to arm the weapon.

E

F-105D on El Uotia, 1962

When F-105Ds first joined two fighter wings of USAF (Europe) their role was to provide an instant nuclear response to attacks from the Soviet bloc. Training for this took place in Europe and in Libya from Wheelus AB. F-105D-15-RE 61-0041 was the aircraft assigned to Col Wilbur J. Grumbles, commander of the 49th TFW at Spangdahlem AB, West Germany, and the first F-105 to arrive on the base when he flew it in on October 30, 1961. It was nicknamed "Kordel-Eden" after a city near the base and Col Grumbles' hometown, Eden in Texas. Here, he is flying it on the El Uotia Bombing Range in Libya on a low-altitude penetration sortie in January 1962.

Maj Aquillan Britt flew 479th TFS F-105D-5-RE 59-1737 "Cherry Boy" to Tan Son Nhut AB to mark his 100th mission. Landing in poor visibility, it collided with an oncoming C-123K transport aircraft on the runway after the latter had aborted a takeoff. The burning F-105 careered down the runway for another 5,000ft, killing its pilot and one of the C-123K crew members. (Don Larsen via Norm Taylor)

PAL had been introduced in 1959 for alert F-100s, and it used a four- or five-digit code, sent by radio, and typed into a small keyboard in the cockpit to arm the weapon.

Periodically and unannounced, practice scrambles would be called. Simulation of getting the authentication codes and going to the aircraft, starting the engines and radioing in would take place. Each pilot had his own real target in a country behind the Iron Curtain and was intimately familiar with it, keeping it on his person while in the alert facility.

Estimating the chances of surviving such a flight, Col Fuller reckoned on

a low percentage, due to the massive number of nuclear strikes planned in East Germany, Czechoslovakia [and other Communist bloc countries]. If you were privy to a map plotting the targets and TOTs you would not want to fly. The main danger would be flash blindness. They included an eye patch in the target folders to cover one eye, so if you lost an eye you'd uncover the patch and still have a good eye! We were also told we could tolerate 25 roentgens of radiation, a figure I would doubt today.

Col Bill Kriz also sat out alerts with the 49th TFW

by flights, every four weeks. Each of the three squadrons provided one flight, and we had four flights per squadron. Alert days were 24 hrs each and you had Monday through to Thursday, or Friday through Sunday. We went out daily to run-up the bird, but with no taxiing because we were loaded with a "nuke." They were "lay-down" weapons, so practice involved a low-level navigation course with a radar delivery. Most were simulated drops, but dummy bombs were dropped at the French range following a low-level navigation route.

F-105Ds carrying Mk 82 and M117 bombs take on fuel during the outbound leg of their mission. The nearer aircraft has a white diamond marking, one of the 469th TFS experimental individual identification symbols prior to the introduction of tail-codes. (Col Jack Spillers via Norm Taylor)

USAFE's relationship with the F-105 was comparatively brief, and the increasing demands of a war far away from Europe hastened its move to the F-4 Phantom II so that USAFE F-105s could be released for service in Thailand. The 36th TFW began transition to the F-4D late in 1965 and the 49th TFW early in 1967. The USAFE wings' task

"Miss Universe/Mary B" (58-1167) of the 34th TFS, 388th TFW had its right horizontal stabilizer shot off by AAA, but it made the 300-mile return journey to a safe recovery at Da Nang. It appears to have a replacement vertical fin from another F-105D, with the reverse camouflage scheme painted on one in four F-105s in 1965. The tan (FS30219) and green (FS 34102) areas of the pattern replaced each other. (Don Larsen via Norm Taylor)

was also complicated by the need to cycle all aircraft through Project Look-Alike, which upgraded their conventional weapons capability among other modifications, including a coat of silver lacquer, during 1962–63.

Many of the USAFE Thunderchiefs were transferred to the 23rd TFW at McConnell AFB, Kansas, which became central to F-105 operations worldwide. From March 1965 it began to rotate squadrons to Southeast Asia, and from January 1, 1966 it became the replacement training unit (RTU) for F-105 crews. In 1968 it added a fourth squadron, the 4519th CCTS, which took over F-105 training from the Nellis-based 4520th CCTW until 1970, when it began to train ANG pilots to fly the F-105. In its last two years until July 1972 it also introduced the F-105D Thunderstick II and deployed its 561st TFS F-105Gs to war.

Thunder in the East

The F-105's crucial role in the Vietnam War began with the arrival of 18 aircraft from the Yokota AB-based 36th TFS at Korat RTAFB on August 12, 1964 in response to the North Vietnamese attack on a US intelligence-gathering ship, the USS *Maddox*. Combat began with attacks on Pathet Lao AAA (antiaircraft artillery) positions as part of a ResCAP effort, and the first loss of an F-105D, scrapped after fire damage while strafing enemy guns. The beginning of Operation *Barrel Roll* on December 10, 1964 brought more 18th TFW Thunderchiefs to Korat to escort USAF reconnaissance flights and conduct limited armed reconnaissance missions from Da Nang AB against infiltration routes in eastern Laos. These early missions showed that the F-105, with limited air-to-air refueling availability, predictably suffered rapid fuel exhaustion when flying at low altitudes with heavy ordnance loads of six M117 bombs or two AGM-12B Bullpup missiles and rocket pods or CBU-2 dispensers. They also indicated that the deterrent effect of America's most potent tactical fighter wasn't enough to curtail North Vietnamese ambitions.

Former F-100 pilot Col Bill Hosmer, who was a member of the Thunderbirds F-100

Korat RTAFB replaced its open flight lines with metal and sand revetment walls in 1966, although the Thai bases were far safer than those in South Vietnam. This F-105D with "Dixie Twister" nose-art plus a "zap" from the 8th TFW at Ubon RTAFB is being prepared to deliver its load of M117s. The "FOD" warning is a reminder of how often fragile turbojet engines were damaged by small pieces of debris. (USAF)

This 469th TFS F-105D-30-RE (62-4269) will soon arrive "on target," living up to its nickname. It was also named "Big Mike," "Okie Judy," "The Impossible Dream," and "Phylus 1" at various times before its combat career ended on April 3, 1969. Maj Peter Christianson was lost when the aircraft was hit by automatic weapons fire during a *Barrel Roll* mission. (USAF)

team, flew with the 12th TFS at Kadena from 1963 and made TDYs (temporary deployments) for Vietnam missions.

> Most of my Thud activity over North Vietnam was low-level delivery of CBU-2s. The wonderful low-level speed of the Thud gave us the only advantage against the gunners, since we were at 200ft for getting that CBU-2 weapon on target. Strafing on the way to the drop also helped to keep their heads down. The "Gatling" [M61A1 gun] was such a fine weapon, and a vast improvement over the F-100's guns.

Col Boyd Van Horn, who checked out in the F-105 in 1963, joined one of the early 562nd TFS TDYs from the 23rd TFW under Operation *Two Buck Nine* at Takhli.

> They lost quite a few pilots in a short time so two of my friends and I volunteered as replacements. We first flew our missions North and recovered at Da Nang. We would then fly another mission out of Da Nang and recover to Takhli for a couple of weeks until we were approved to fly unrestricted out of Thailand.

As the US response intensified, F-105s began Operation *Steel Tiger* missions against Laotian targets on April 11, 1965, and night attacks on North Vietnamese transport routes. The nature of the terrain, North Vietnamese skill in camouflaging, and the crippling limits of the US Rules of Engagement severely limited the F-105 pilots' success rate. Often, "flak traps" would be set up, using a damaged truck placed conspicuously on a jungle trail to lure pilots into concentrated antiaircraft fire. The statistics were unpromising, with an average of six F-105 sorties required to destroy each truck. Bob Cooley was one of many pilots who questioned the logic of this:

> strafing a $20,000 truck with a multimillion dollar airplane. Why didn't we just call up there and buy the trucks?

Laotian operations against the transportation trails expanded under a variety of code names. *Tiger Hound*, from December 1965, required F-105s to fly with forward air control (FAC) O-1E spotter planes manned by USAF and Laotian aircrew. They flew vertigo-inducing Gate Guard night sorties, with targets illuminated by flares from C-130 transports and, from 1966, Combat Skyspot missions, in which formations of F-105s bombed from straight and level flight above cloud, guided by radar sites up to 190 miles away from the target. Targets that were already well-disguised by jungle forest stretching to 200ft in height were made even less accessible by the dense monsoon cloud-base that covered much of North Vietnam from November to

April. Although Laos remained clearer during that time, Combat Skyspot was used over both areas.

Operation *Rolling Thunder*, which gave the F-105 its most prominent role, began as a "graduated response" to North Vietnam's attacks on US bases and an attempt to force a negotiated settlement. It was hoped that several weeks of attacks beginning on March 2, 1965 would force the North to back down. The campaign was finally abandoned 44 months later when it became clear that Hanoi had no such intentions. The main strike components in this phase of the air war were the two F-105 wings based in Thailand. The 355th TFW, which had begun conversion to the F-105 in 1962, was assigned permanent change of station (PCS) with its three F-105 squadrons to Takhli RTAFB from George AFB in November 1965. At Korat RTAFB, 155 miles from Takhli, the reactivated 388th TFW built up to four F-105 squadrons from April/May 1966. Both wings replaced provisional wings that had managed temporary deployments by a number of F-105 units since April 1964.

For the first phase of the air war, many F-105 pilots had long experience of the aircraft from their time in PACAF or USAFE. Bill Kriz recalls:

One departed from Spangdahlem upon completion of a tour and one was sent to either F-105 base [Takhli or Korat]. In my case, Spangdahlem was about to convert to the F-4 Phantom II, so I was able to curtail my tour and volunteer for Southeast Asia in the '105. I preferred going to combat in a bird that I had flown for 800 hours rather than converting to the F-4 and eventually going there anyway in a strange aircraft. By that time (late 1966) everyone who hadn't been to Southeast Asia was on the hook to go eventually.

Bob Cooley:

We were all trained and current in all the weapons delivery techniques, so that's why they came to the USAFE bases for crews. There was no specific [war] theater preparation until we got there. My first mission was the second time I flew from Takhli.

Several Thailand-based F-105 wing commanders often came from USAFE backgrounds. Col John Giraudo succeeded Col William Chairsell as 49th TFW commander and both went on to command the 355th and 388th TFWs respectively. Bill Kriz recalled how in 1967

Col Giraudo was reassigned from Spangdahlem to Takhli. On the way he stopped off at Korat and assembled all former "Spang" jocks for an informal meeting to discuss

"Big Kahuna," F-105D-20-RE 61-0109, was assigned to Col John C. Giraudo during his time as commander of the 355th TFW in 1967–68, and shared his nickname. It was lost while making a fourth strafing pass against a storage area on the Plain of Jars on March 2, 1969. (Robert Archer collection)

The crew chief of F-105D-25-RE 61-0220 prepares Maj Jack Spillers' cockpit for another mission from Korat. It was the first of two "Jeanie" F-105Ds named after the pilot's wife. (Lt Col Jack Spillers via Norm Taylor)

the tactics situation. That shows the type he was, to rely on his former jocks for information.

Boyd Van Horn:

I arrived at Bitburg in late 1965 and was assigned to the 53rd TFS commanded by Sandy Vandenberg. My old ops officer, Jim Kasler, was there, along with a bunch of friends from Turner AFB. They all volunteered to go to Southeast Asia and most went to Takhli.

As operations officer for the 354th TFS at Takhli, Maj Kasler led one of the most devastating F-105 attacks on North Vietnam's fuel storage areas on June 29, 1966. He became the only person to receive the Air Force Cross three times, and he was an inspiring leader during his 78 months as a PoW in Hanoi after being shot down on August 8, 1966 at a time when 11 F-105s were lost in a single week.

When the first *Rolling Thunder* strikes hit ammunition dumps in southern North Vietnam, F-105s were accompanied by F-100 Super Sabre MiGCAP (combat air patrol) and flak-suppression flights, or SVAF A-1 Skyraiders with the F-105s and F-100s providing flak suppression for these piston-engined bombers. For these mid-March 1965 attacks, the Thunderchiefs carried 2.75in. rocket pods, CBU-2 cluster bomb dispensers and, for the first time, napalm canisters. By March 22, the F-105s were flying without the SVAF and attacking early-warning radar sites, and the following month saw the F-100 escorts replaced by the newly arrived F-4C Phantom IIs of the 45th TFS at Ubon RTAFB. It also marked the beginning of Phase II of *Rolling Thunder*.

From April 3, 1965 the emphasis of the widening campaign was on North Vietnamese transport, particularly its many road and rail bridges. Bombing and reattacking bridges because the structures were so stubbornly solid became one of the F-105 units' most important roles, costing many aircraft and crews. The first major bridge target was the massive, 540ft-long "Dragon's Jaw" (Ham Rong) structure at Than Hoa. Forty-six F-105s hit it with M117 bombs and AGM-12A Bullpups on April 3, but even this weight of ordnance caused only surface damage. Mission commander Lt Col Robinson Risner at Korat replaced the Bullpups with M117s for a reattack the following day, which cost three F-105s, two of them the first US aircraft to be shot down by VPAF (Vietnamese Peoples' Air Force) MiGs in air-to-air combat. Despite more than 300 hits, the huge steel and concrete structure still stood and became North Vietnam's most heavily defended, and often-attacked, target until felled by 3,000lb laser-guided bombs in May 1972.

The accuracy of the F-105 pilots was seldom in doubt despite the heaviest local air defenses in the history of air warfare, but the ordnance was often inadequate for such heavily engineered targets in 1965. More spectacular results were achieved on August 11, 1967 when the 8,437ft Paul Doumer Bridge, the longest in North Vietnam, was finally cleared for attack. F-105s from the 355th TFW had their standard M117 bombs replaced by a centerline fuel tank and a 3,000lb M118 bomb under each wing. Dropping both these massive weapons simultaneously was essential, because if one bomb "hung up" the asymmetric load would immediately throw the fighter out of control. Col Giraudo chose his most experienced pilots since the target was close to central Hanoi and very heavily defended. They were joined by F-105Ds from the 388th TFW, flak-suppression flights from both wings, and a flight of

F-105F Wild Weasels from Korat. F-4C Phantom IIs from the 8th TFW led by Col Robin Olds supplied MiGCAP and also participated in the bombing. In all, 94 tons of ordnance was delivered, destroying one railway and two road spans of the bridge. No aircraft were lost. After repairs to the structure F-105s were called back for successful reattacks in October and December 1967.

By 1967, tactics for F-105-based strike packages for the heavily defended Route Pack VIA targets in North Vietnam were well established. Using formations that derived from USAAF bombing in World War II, a strike package usually had four or eight flights (16 or 32 aircraft) of F-105D bombers, and one or two flights of F-105F flak suppressors. MiGs were kept at bay by two F-4 Phantom II flights, and support aircraft included eight KC-135A tankers flying in "racetrack" patterns over Laos or the Gulf of Tonkin, several EB-66 radar jamming aircraft, and various radar/communications aircraft such as the Lockheed EC-121 circling offshore to monitor enemy defenses and warn of imminent attacks. In the background was a network of rescue helicopters and A-1 Skyraiders to provide armed cover for search and rescue. In-flight refueling usually took place soon after the aircraft took off and joined formation, and again after leaving hostile airspace. If pilots were required to fly cover for a downed aircrew, they would probably need several more top-ups.

Ordnance loads depended on the target, but as Col Bill Kriz recalled

> Most of our bomb loads consisted of six 750lb M117s on the centerline rack for a normal strike mission. When going up north (Pack VI) the lead and No 3 aircraft carried the AIM-9 Sidewinder. Everyone had an ECM pod, or at least the lead and No 3 did. I carried 3,000lb bombs on ten missions and 1,000lb bombs on six.

The introduction of ECM pods was an urgent response to the heavy losses of F-105s (126 from Korat and Takhli in 1966 alone), some of which were due to SA-2 missiles and radar-directed antiaircraft fire. The QRC-160A (ALQ-71) pods that started to arrive in Thailand in mid-1966 were tuned to jam the SA-2 "Guideline" missile's "Fan Song" guidance radar and the

Lt Col Spillers took over command of the 357th TFS at Takhli in 1969 and had a second Thunderchief, 62-4229, decorated as "I Dream of Jeanie II." He went on to complete 220 combat missions. (Lt Col Jack Spillers via Norm Taylor)

Lt Karl Richter had already completed 100 missions north when he destroyed a MiG-17F flown by Do Huy Hoang on September 21, 1966. Sadly, Richter himself was shot down just short of his 200th mission on July 28, 1967. (USAF)

"Firecan" radar used to control the heavy 57mm and 85mm AAA.

In operational trials each Thunderchief carried a pod on each outboard pylon for the best coverage of hostile radiation frequencies, but the increasing MiG threat and a shortage of pods required one pylon for an AIM-9B missile. For the pilot, the only job was to switch pods on or off, but because a "Fan Song" could "see through" the pod's coverage inside 8 miles' range, the F-105s adopted "pod formation" to maximize the jamming effect. This meant virtually straight and level flight in a formation, with set distances between aircraft in high threat areas. If the flight banked beyond 15 degrees the jamming pattern lost strength. Bill Kriz explains:

Pod formation was pretty easy. We basically flew a "loose close" and tried to stay within 1,000ft of each other. We approached the target at altitude at 450kts. By the time we rolled in and dropped we were close to supersonic. That had a lot to do with not being hit. On most sorties up north we had an F-4 MiGCAP, and I never had any MiG attacks that required jettisoning the ordnance. On a typical Pack VI sortie the AAA started as soon as the lead aircraft rolled in [to dive bomb]. I don't recall much flak while we were straight and level at altitude.

He narrowly avoided AAA while on his 100th mission, flown with MiG killer "Mo" Seaver, "Bear" Chambers, and Bob Piper, who were also on their 100th and consequent end-of-tour missions. It was in Route Pack V.

It should have been relatively safe, but it was the closest I came to being hit. On the way "down the chute" [to attack] a red fireball passed within ten feet of my windscreen at 12 o'clock.

The enormous weight of enemy AAA accounted for the majority of F-105 losses, particularly at lower altitudes, and with the irony of fate a number of pilots were shot down on their 99th or 100th mission. The pilots' goal was 100 missions – they even had a song about it. The limit initially was 100 combat missions, but this was changed in 1965 to 100 missions over North Vietnam. As F-105 veteran Ben Fuller pointed out, only 63 percent completed their 100.

Tactics using the ECM pods highlighted basic differences in attack profiles between the Korat and Takhli wings. As Col Kriz explained,

F-105D in combat, Vietnam, 1967

Maj Ralph L. Kuster of the 13th TFS, 388th TFW was No 2 aircraft in Hambone flight of F-105Ds, leading an attack on the Bac Giang transportation hub near Hanoi on June 3, 1967. Kuster bombed a heavy AAA site, then sighted three MiG-17s, which Hambone turned to engage 6 miles from the target. Capt Larry D. Wiggins in F-105D Hambone 03 destroyed one with an AIM-9B missile and 20mm gunfire. Kuster turned behind the leading MiG-17, firing a stream of 20mm shells from his F-105D, "Mickey Titty Chi" (60-0424), ahead of its flight path. The burning MiG crashed inverted, killing its pilot (probably Lt Phan Tan Duan). This was the time of highest losses for the VPAF, with 32 MiGs claimed by US pilots in May–June 1967.

F-105D-5-REs from the first production batch remained in service throughout the war, like "Jo Ann" (58-1172) of the 34th TFS, seen at Udorn in 1968 and also known as "Daisy Mae/Stud Thud." It received all the updates to the vertical fin intake, fuselage-side air-scoops, and AN/APR-25 ECM additions of F-105D-31-RE models. Postwar it flew with the District of Columbia ANG until 1976. (USAF)

Korat flew into high-threat areas at altitude (21–22,000ft) and dive-bombed targets from there. Takhli used low-level, high-speed approach to the target with a pop-up maneuver to about 12,000ft and bombed from there.

Brig Gen Chairsell, commanding the 388th TFW at the time, believed that the pods could be relied upon to protect the attackers at altitude, whereas F-105s were more vulnerable to AAA when approaching at low altitude. In Bob Kriz's opinion, each approach had its good and bad points, although Col Jack Broughton, vice commander at Takhli, attributed Korat's higher loss rate in 1966–67 partly to their tactics, which were advocated by the PACAF commander, Gen John Ryan.

The MiG Threat

With such intensive mission rates (the 355th TFW passed its 100,000th combat flying hour in April 1968), encounters with North Vietnam's small but determined force of MiG defenders inevitably increased. MiG pilots were directed to avoid the escorting Phantom IIs and shoot down the F-105 bombers, or at least disrupt their formations and force them to jettison their ordnance and defend themselves or escape. With all the advantages of effective Soviet-designed ground-control networks, proximity to home bases and light, nimble fighters, the MiG pilots could be directed to positions from which they could ambush incoming American jets from altitudes below US radar coverage and evade the CAP fighters. The F-105s were at their most vulnerable as they pulled off target after bombing. Separated from the rest of their flight and accelerating to regain altitude, they could be intercepted by well-directed MiGs. Capt Bob "Spade" Cooley was No 3 in a flight of F-105Ds on December 14, 1966, a day when seven US aircraft were lost. The No 4 man in his flight had the disadvantage of a heavy documentary camera pod on one pylon, which provided combat film for the intelligence community but slowed down the element as it pulled off target. Bob Cooley:

> I had been hit by flak several times heading into Hanoi. It sounded like hard hail hitting the sides of the airframe. We were bombing the [Yen Vien] railyards and I could see the needles on two of my hydraulic systems start to waver and the stick was getting a little heavy. So I popped up and bombed and then headed out as the airplane started to "freeze up."

As he did so, a MiG-21 (Red 4212) flown by 921st Fighter Regiment pilot Senior Lt Dong Van De dived from 6,000ft above the F-105, with the sun behind him, and fired an "Atoll" missile, which detonated inside the J75 engine, causing a huge explosion. His wingman, top VPAF ace Nguyen Van Coc, shouted, "It's burning. A good kill!" Capt Cooley ejected as the F-105 fragmented around him, finding to his surprise that he still had his throttle lever in his hand as he descended by parachute ("I wish I'd kept it," he commented to the author), and landed in jungle trees.

> I had been bashed around pretty hard. I reached up to get my helmet off and the whole thing just crumbled in my hands. The only thing holding it together was the leather liner. It had done its job, as my head wasn't hurt at all apart from a slight cut on the chin where the oxygen mask came off. The helmet had hit the canopy bow on the way out.

He landed on a small hill and awaited rescue.

> Col Broughton [who managed the rescue effort] had almost 50 airplanes over that hill. He was cycling people to tankers and getting them to save their cannon ammunition.

An HH-3E helicopter appeared over Bob as he hid in undergrowth deep in hostile territory, while four A-1 Sandy aircraft held off the North Vietnamese, who had advanced to within 50ft of his position.

> They got the tree penetrator [rescue hoist] to me and started to winch me up, and as I was looking up I could see all kinds of flashes along the bottom of the helicopter where it was being hit by small-arms fire. I expected a helicopter on my head any minute.

Bob returned to base with a back injury. Lt Dong Van De was lost in action on June 11, 1967.

Bob Cooley remembers one of his Takhli commanders, Col Robert Ray Scott, as "quite a character." He had scored three victories at night in World War II as a P-61 Black Widow pilot, had flown 117 F-86 Sabre missions in Korea, and took over the 355th TFW in August 1966. Leading by example, he flew another 135 combat missions as commander and made the eighth F-105 MiG kill of the war on March 26, 1967 while attacking a target near the Hoa Lac MiG base, northwest of Hanoi. Col Scott had led his flight as it delivered its bomb load and as he pulled up at 4,000ft he noticed a MiG-17 taking off from the Hoa Lac runway, putting itself within the Rules of Engagement as a legitimate target rather than "out of bounds" as it would have been when on the ground. He managed to turn inside the MiG (quite an achievement in an F-105) and shredded its left wing with gunfire. Another MiG kill was marked up on his F-105D 59-1772 a month later when Maj Harry Higgins flew it as lead aircraft in Spitfire flight, attacking the Han Phong causeway near Hanoi on what proved to be very much a "MiG day." Two flights of MiG-17s had been vectored to intercept the F-105s as they came off

A 354th TFS flight led by F-105D-10-RE (60-0490), also known as "Captain Radio," heads for a Ho Chi Minh trails target in October 1969, with Mk 84 and Mk 82 bombs fitted with "daisy cutter" fuse extensions. Looking for a hole in the clouds was often the only way to acquire a target visually. Against RP6 targets, the 355th TFW tactic was usually to approach the target at around 4,500ft, "pop up" to about 12,000ft, and roll the aircraft inverted to see the target. Rolling out and diving from this "perch" position, the pilot would then release bombs at 4,000ft and "jink" as he regained altitude for egress. (USAF)

target. Maj Higgins saw a MiG at his 2 o'clock position and turned towards it. Proving that a skillfully flown F-105 could duel to some extent with nimble MiG-17s, he reported that he engaged in a series of turning maneuvers, finally gaining the 6 o'clock position on its tail.

Because the F-105's weapons controls were usually set for bombing, it required some complex switching operations to change to Sidewinder or "guns" in an air-to-air situation. The gunsight also had to be adjusted for gunfire rather than bombing, and most pilots tended to "hose" the cannon at a MiG target without using the sight in order to grab an opportunity. Harry Higgins managed to get a Sidewinder set up while he was hauling his F-105 into the advantageous tail-chase position. He advanced to about 3,000ft behind the MiG and fired his AIM-9B

The MiG immediately tightened his turn to the right and the missile missed by 1,000ft. By this time my wingman, 1st Lt Gordon Jenkins, had regained excellent position [formation] and we continued our turn to the west for egress from the area. Rolling out westerly, we immediately spotted two MiG-17s in our 1 o'clock position. As the MiGs approached in a head-on pass, we could see that they were firing cannon. As the closure distance decreased, we also fired bursts at the MiGs without any visible damage. We turned to pursue the MiGs. However, they continued southeast and were well out of range as we fell into their 6 o'clock position.

Again we turned to egress and I spotted a single MiG in a left turn, heading south. I immediately turned into the enemy and engaged afterburner for closure. I completed the switch settings for guns and began to close. The MiG tightened his turn but was slow in doing so. This allowed me to gain a 30-degree cut-off angle, and when I was approximately 1,500ft behind I began to fire the 20mm cannon. As I prolonged the firing, I noticed the MiG begin to smoke and flames erupted from his left wing-root section. He began a steep, descending turn with the left wing down. I positioned myself for another firing pass but we were forced to break hard right to offset two more MiGs that were firing at us from 1,000ft in our 5–6 o'clock position. The MiGs chased us at high speed until we finally out-distanced them by applying negative-G forces and obtaining a great amount of airspeed. My last glance at the MiG that I had hit showed him burning and spiraling towards the ground at less than 500ft.

F-105 pilots went on to score 22.5 MiG-17s in 1967, adding to the five destroyed the previous year. Three were shot down by two-seat F-105Fs, one being shared with an F-4D crew. Only two were AIM-9B kills, the rest relied on the M61A1 cannon. All showed the versatility of the F-105 "bomber" and the skill of men who saw themselves very much as fighter pilots.

Weaseling On

Attrition and TAC's progressive introduction of F-4/RF-4 Phantom IIs meant that F-105Ds were among the first combat aircraft to be withdrawn under President Nixon's "draw-down" of US forces from 1969. However, the specialized F-105F/G Wild Weasel continued to play a crucial role up to the end of hostilities in September 1973. After the F-105F Wild Weasel III's combat debut in May 1966, it was used to lead search and destroy missions against SA-2s in which an F-105F would lead two or three bomb-carrying F-105Ds. As Bob Cooley recalled, "we went at the direction of the Weasel leader who would spot the targets." At Korat the Wild Weasel flight was operated by the 13th TFS, with 12 converted F-105Fs on strength by September 1966. Takhli chose to spread their Weasels as a separate flight within each of the three F-105 squadrons from July 4, 1966. As Ben Fuller explained

F-105G-1-RE 63-8291 "Mutley the Flying Dog" of the 17th WWS was at Korat RTAFB in August 1973 when Congress pulled the financial plug on the Vietnam War in order to end American involvement. The last F-105Gs then returned to the USA in October, ending ten years of F-105 wartime commitment. (Larsen/Remington via Norm Taylor)

Nose-art that appeared on both sides of F-105D 62-4286 of the 469th TFS. This aircraft fell victim to an SA-2 missile during a mission near Hanoi on November 6, 1967 in which its pilot, Maj Robert Hagerman, was killed. (via Norm Taylor)

We were administratively in all three squadrons. In 1967 we had very few Weasel F-105Fs, so a Weasel would be scheduled in the Nos 1 and 3 positions, with F-105Ds flown by regular "strike" pilots. Weasel pilots very rarely flew F-105Ds. I had one F-105D flight in 100 sorties when my "bear" [back-seater] was sick. At Takhli the senior Weasel pilot (Leo Thorsness when I was there) did the scheduling. Weasels were left on their own to design tactics and identify areas to work and attack. The best intelligence was to talk to the last crews to fly. We posted "hot" SA-2 sites on a map in the planning room.

As numbers were rebuilt, four Weasels preceded each strike package as two elements, circling near SAM sites to draw the missile batteries' fire from the F-105D bombers and locate the exact source of the radar emissions from each site.

Weasels took off first and rendezvoused with the KC-135 tankers, then flew over Laos into North Vietnam. We were normally 3 to 5 minutes or 30 miles ahead of the strike force, and therefore the first to report back to them on weather and alerts on SAM and AAA activity. We would be in the target area for about 20 minutes or so at 550 to 600kts, pulling 3–4G. We were very exhausted and sweaty when we got home after an average mission of 3.5 to 4 hours.

Attacks could be made with Shrike missiles, CBU, and bombs. Weasel crews then had to out-maneuver any SAMs that were fired at them by a series of exactly timed high-G "split-S" dives and climbs. It was an extremely risky procedure and losses were high, with four F-105Fs downed in July and August 1967, leaving a single Weasel F-105F at Takhli by August 7. For Ben Fuller

the worst mission was on April 30, 1967 when I was leading inbound to the target and MiGs popped up from below us and shot down my No 3 man, Leo Thorsness, and his EWO Harry Johnson, and also the No 4, Bob Abbott in an F-105D.

The target was Hanoi's thermal power station, already severely damaged the previous day. The mission was jinxed from the outset, starting with an untraceable, jammed rescue beeper that went off in someone's parachute pack on takeoff and emitted a shrill sound for most of the mission.

Ben and his EWO Norm Frith were leading Carbine flight of Weasels ahead of the strike flights, looking for SAMs. Leo Thorsness and Harry Johnson were flying another F-105F as Carbine 3.

As Weasels, Leo and Harry were like brothers. Ironically, as our Weasel leader, Leo scheduled who flew and in what positions. He had already flown a mission that morning and when the regular pilot was not well he put himself into the No 3 slot. At the time Carbine was attacked, there were no SA-2 launches and no SAM radars were even "up." Before that it had just been random "looks" [by enemy radars]. We weren't even in range of any potential SA-2 sites. We all had a feeling that some missions were SAM days and some were MiG days, based on the number of SAM sites that would be "up."

April 30 was to be a MiG day. Carbine flight was up to 20 miles ahead of the strike force and its F-4 MiGCAP escorts, one of which may have detected two "Atoll" missiles heading for Carbine but mistaken them for SA-2s. Another pilot probably misidentified a flight of aircraft behind Carbine as American jets. The weight of radio traffic and the stuck beeper made it hard to tell. In retrospect, it became clear that a flight of MiG-21s, including two piloted by top VPAF aces Nguyen Ngoc Do and Nguyen Van Coc, with a third flown by Le Trong Huyen, was orbiting at low level, out of radar, beneath the F-105s' approach path. Ben Fuller:

It amazes me that more VPAF pilots didn't use that tactic. It is something I would have done. Our strike forces were so predictable that it didn't take the best and most cunning to know where we would be and when. We flew two main strikes every day from Korat or Takhli and we all went over Channel 97 or Northern Laos to cross the Red River at a similar point on the way to Thud Ridge and then to the target. We wanted to use terrain masking where possible. The VPAF could have a relaxing breakfast and be looking for us between 8 and 9 in the morning and 4 and 5 in the afternoon. It was only different when we went up the Gulf of Tonkin and attacked the northeast railroad from the east.

"Atoll" missiles from the MiG-21s hit 1st Lt Bob Abbott's F-105D, Carbine 4 (which had lagged slightly behind the formation), forcing him to eject, and fatally damaged Carbine 3. Leo Thorsness called, "I've flamed out. Mayday, Mayday, Mayday," and ejected from his burning F-105F with Harry Johnson. Strike leader Col Broughton immediately turned the mission over to a search and rescue effort, but the "bad day at Black River," as Ben Fuller called it, wasn't nearly over. A tragic combination of interrupted and misunderstood communications between the strike and rescue forces, coupled

After a full combat career, including time with the 357th TFS as "Thor's Hammer" and "Road Runner," F-105G-1-RE 63-8339 flew with the 128th TFS, Georgia ANG, which accepted some of the 35th TFW's Weasels and flew them until May 1983, ending 20 years of ANG service for the "Thud." (via A. Thornborough)

with helicopters' mechanical problems and disproportionate amounts of bad luck, meant that a heroic rescue effort failed to prevent these three pilots and a fourth, Capt Joseph Abbott, being captured. Capt Abbott's F-105D was also felled by an "Atoll" as he left the rescue scene.

F-4 escort missions outside RP6 could be hazardous too. Maj Warren Kerzon and his "bear," Lt Col Scott McIntire, experienced "the most intense, most terrifying, most exciting 40 seconds of our combat experience" in Route Pack 1 on May 19, 1968 in F-105F 63-8311 (later nicknamed "SAM Fighter"). Flying cover for Cadillac flight of Ubon F-4Ds, which was making its last bombing pass, they suddenly picked up a 3.5-ring "Fan Song" warning on their APR-25, closely followed by a red launch warning light from SAM site "Lead 89." Kerzon recalls:

The signal is on the nose. A four-ring SAM! Doppler shows seven miles. I mash down on the "pickle" button and my portside Shrike roars off the wing. It streaks out smartly, straight as a string for about one second, then dips sharply earthward, homing on a very strong signal. I ripple off my second Shrike. It does the same.

Still in burner, I yank over to the left and spot two separate yellow-orange "Bee-bees" below. Within a short time they turn bright white. I transmit again, "SAMs airborne, Lead 89." I push down and turn a bit but they stay locked on a spot inside my right windscreen. They are closing fast. How do I judge their slant range? Impossible. I am thinking (foolishly) at this point, "If I don't make the right move at the right time, Scottie is dead". It did not dawn on me until the next day that – swell – I'm sitting here some 30 inches in front of Scottie! Weird, what runs through your mind.

Suddenly I see a distinct divergence of the two SAMs, with forward movement by the one closest to my nose. I make a rolling left pull-up, both SAMs disappear below my nose. Number 1 SAM flashes by my left side. The glow of its sustainer engine is blinding. I think I flinched at this point and assumed a fetal position over the control stick. Scottie sees a flash from the No 1 SAM. I rolled right back, pushing the nose down, still in burner, and picked up No 2 SAM. I pushed over to get it into better view – what's this? A No 3 SAM coming up fast to the right of No 2. With this surprise, I pushed a healthy negative "G." With that rather abrupt maneuver, both SAMs moved rapidly, high over the canopy, nearly in formation, at a closing speed of 3,000ft per second. Scottie called out, "The signal's down, no sweat," about 5 seconds after the SAMs went by. He thought he felt a "whumping" as they passed.

On return to Takhli, they found a hole drilled clean through the aft section of their F-105 by SAM shrapnel, but they also had the gratifying news that the SAM site had been put out of action by their Shrike attack.

The last phase of the Thunderchiefs' war was fought by the final F-105G version. Although Mod O F-105Fs had performed combat trials of the AMG-78A, the April 1968 bombing halt curtailed activities over North Vietnam, and F-105Fs reverted to bombing missions over the "trails" (often in single-pilot configuration) and ECM support for B-52 Arc Light strikes. Boyd Van Horn recalled flying "cover for B-52s at night in the Mu Gia Pass when we had their bombs go through our formation [at much lower altitude than the B-52s] several times because of poor co-ordination between the 'BUFFs' and us."

Maj Kerzon and Lt Col McIntire had flown the first combat mission with the AGM-78A on March 10, 1968. "Finally we had something that could out-shoot the SA-2. The Standard ARM could reach out and touch you from 60 miles away. Mister SAM was in for a big surprise." The crew had tested the missile against simulated North Vietnamese radars at Eglin AFB and they briefed the project pilot, George Acree, on the system. He then flew one of the four Barracuda flight aircraft with AGM-78s. As they approached Hanoi in poor weather, the EWOs

began to pick up every type of electronic signal from the North Vietnamese air defense system: "Bar Lock," "Low Blow," "Cross Slot," "Fire Can," and "Fan Song" – the Bad

A 465th TFS "Sooners" F-105D- 31-RE returns from a sortie, advancing in a way that seems to cause consternation to the lady onlookers in the background. Its service life began with the 8th TFW at Itazuke AB in 1963 and ended in 1984 when it was transferred to the March Field Air Museum, California. (Author's collection)

Guys knew we were inbound. While I scanned the skies for MiGs Scottie focused on the visual and audio signals coming from his magic black boxes. Above the hum of our J75 engine the only sounds inside our trusty Thud were the squeaks and squawks of the incoming hostile signals and our steady, heavy breathing.

The Phantom II strike force weather-aborted, leaving Barracuda flight to press on.

We had the "hungries" for a SAM kill. Our plan was simple. We would nose up to the SAM sites on the south side of Hanoi, close enough to get the enemy sites to come up on the air, but not so close (about 25 miles) as to "spook" them into turning off their radar.

The first three AGM-78s were launched, but one had motor failure and two others disintegrated soon after launch. Then flight leader Harley Wyman fired his missiles, with better luck:

scoring good ignitions, good trajectories, against strong signals. SAMs pop out of the overcast in front of us, unguided – no threat. Black puffs of 85mm or 100mm flak above us. We are beginning to piss them off! Scottie calls, "Got a steady green [hostile radar emission], two o'clock – fire when ready, Gridley!" I squirt off my last missile – "thump" – ignition, good trajectory. When fired against a maximum range target, the AGM-78 would climb to 80,000ft before diving into its target at high Mach.

Subsequent intelligence-gathering indicated that the five successfully launched missiles scored "three confirmed kills and two 'probables'. At least one missile motored clear across Hanoi onto the north side of town." Barracuda flight had eluded 12 SAMs and Warren later heard that "our second missile had scored a direct hit on the target SAM van site, destroying it and killing its crew. which included four Soviet air defense advisors."

The first F-105Gs began operations from Takhli in mid-1969, moving to Korat when F-105s left Takhli at the end of 1970 after 101,304 combat sorties against 12,675 targets, which included 20 MiGs destroyed in the air and eight on the ground. With the 6010th WWS they took part in the Son Tay POW rescue attempt, and later, as the 17th WWS, continued to support Arc Light and reconnaissance flights during 1971. Bombing of the North resumed in April 1972 in Operation *Linebacker I*, when F-105Gs flew as hunter-killer teams with F-4E Phantoms, and continued through the *Linebacker II* raids of Christmas 1972. McConnell AFB sent its 561st TFS with more F-105Gs to share the 17th WWS missions from Korat. Lt Col Barry Miller was the squadron's intelligence officer at the time, and he recalled some of the new challenges of this last phase of the "battle of the beams" for F-105G crews, including optically guided SAMs using a "radar-less" visual tracker mounted on the "Fan Song F" radar van. The dual Shrike launcher using an ADU-315/316 adapter allowed all F-105Gs to carry pairs of Shrikes on their outer pylons. However,

it was not popular with pilots. It produced increased drag, and at least one case where a Shrike failed to separate gave it a bad reputation. Even one of its early advocates, the 17th WWS, turned against it by mid-1972.

There was also the "Black SAM" crisis in 1972, when it was feared that North Vietnam had received new missiles, possibly the Soviet SA-4 and the

T8029 radar from China, all of which would require new tactics and technology to defeat. These fears were soon allayed and attributed to sightings of SA-2s with unfamiliar camouflage.

> Somehow the dark paint scheme made the missile look different in flight to the crews who were used to seeing gray SA-2s. They also felt the missile maneuvered differently. Finally, we recovered warhead fragments from an F-105G damaged by a reported "Black SAM" and analysis revealed them to be from a standard SA-2.

Sadly, the optical "Fan Song F" technique proved fatal for Lt Col Scott McIntire on December 10, 1971. He was the EWO in F-105G 63-8326 with pilot Maj Bob Belli, supporting a B-52 strike near the Mu Gia Pass where SA-2 sites had been detected in southern Laos. Warren Kerzon:

> Bob and Scottie were working a "Fan Song" signal at their 12 o'clock. Scottie picked up a "launch" signal that was not synced with the signal in front of them. Their wingman called a SAM coming up and Bob started a turn to pick it up visually. The next thing Bob recalls is tumbling through the sky with no aircraft behind him, just the cockpit plus him and Scottie. He called for Scottie to eject but Scottie was slumped over with

This 469th TFS Thud line-up includes a few war veterans, one of them (61-0069) a MiG-killer for Capt Larry Wiggins on June 3, 1967. F-105F 63-8331 was one of the few F-105Fs that wasn't sent to Southeast Asia, and F-105D 61-0099 similarly spent most of its time with Stateside units after an initial period with the 49th TFW at Spangdahlem, as did several of the others here. (USAF) no response. Bob ejected, which blew Scottie out first. The Jolly Greens [helicopters] got Bob out that day and a para-rescue man got close enough to Scottie to declare him KIA. The post-mission brief established that they had been hit by an optically guided SAM, so there was no "Fan Song" signal from the side, only a launch light that wasn't synced with the tracking signal [from another site] ahead of them.

When the last 17th WWS F-105Gs returned from Thailand in October 1974, the surviving Thunderchiefs had already entered the final stage of their service. The 23rd TFW ended F-105 operations in July 1972, and in 1973 both F-4 and F-105 Wild Weasel activities were centralized at George AFB, California, with the 35th TFW up to 1980. The 561st TFS was joined by the 17th WWS as the 562nd TFS from October 1974, making several deployments to Europe. Weasel development work continued with the 57th FWW at Nellis AFB until 1975 when it too moved to George AFB.

Later Life

Maj Frank Bernard's "The Desert Fox," an F-105D-31-RE 62-4299 of the 466th TFS at Hill AFB, Utah, with an experimental tan wrap-around scheme applied in the F-105's final year of service. This aircraft spent four years in Southeast Asia with the 355th and 18th TFWs. (T. Shia)

Thunderchiefs had entered Air National Guard service in 1964 when surviving 4th TFW and Thunderbirds F-105Bs began a remarkable 17 years as combat-ready fighter-bombers with the New Jersey ANG. As war-weary F-105Ds returned from Southeast Asia, they too were reallocated to ANG and Air Force Reserve (AFRES) units to have their war wounds healed for further service. In 1971 the District of Columbia ANG received and refurbished ex-355th TFW aircraft that served them for another decade and made a 1976 Coronet Fife NATO deployment to the UK. The Kansas ANG received

F-105Ds from January 1971 and, as the 184th Tactical Fighter Training Group, took over F-105 training from the 23rd TFW until it converted to the F-4D Phantom II in 1979. Virginia's ANG, the 192nd Tactical Fighter Group, flew F-105D/Fs for ten years from 1971, joining the 1976 Coronet Fife deployment and making regular visits to Red Flag exercises. The last F-105 unit was the Georgia ANG, which took over the 35th TFW's F-105F/Gs in 1978, refurbished them thoroughly and flew them until May 25, 1983.

Within AFRES, Carswell AFB, Texas took over the small force of F-105D T-Stick IIs for its 457th TFS in July 1972, exercising its "ready to deploy" status with a NATO visit to Norvenich AB, Germany in 1977 and eventually converting to the Phantom II in 1981. Also at Norvenich in 1977 were F-105Ds of the 465th TFS at Tinker AFB, Oklahoma, which operated "SH"-coded Thunderchiefs from May 1972 until late 1980. F-105Bs also had an AFRES career with the 466th TFS from 1973 until 1980, when F-105D/Fs replaced them. During that time they deployed to Hawaii twice for exercises, and when F-105Ds became available they were taken to Denmark for a 1981 NATO deployment, the last for the F-105. As the last F-105 operator, the squadron gradually exchanged its "HI"-coded Thunderchiefs for F-16A Vipers in 1984, ending the F-105's 26 years with the USAF.

CONCLUSION

The Cold War gave rise to a generation of tactical aircraft that were larger than conventional fighters, able to fly long-range, low-altitude interdiction missions, and capable of providing a second level of nuclear response to support the "big stick" of heavy bombers and missiles. Such aircraft might also have to double as close-support attackers against smaller battlefield targets if necessary, a role later fulfilled by designs like the Thunderchief's direct successor, the Fairchild A-10 Thunderbolt II. This philosophy gave rise to specialized attack bombers like the Hawker-Siddeley Buccaneer, BAC TSR 2, and Panavia Tornado in Europe, and the Grumman A-6 Intruder and General Dynamics F-111 in the USA, although the latter was briefly promoted as a fighter before settling into its true role as an outstanding long-range attacker. Their common features were high speed and excellent stability at low altitude, advanced avionics for night and all-weather interdiction, and usually a two-man crew to share a heavy workload.

The F-105 was therefore a transitional design, combining features of the earlier single-seat attack fighters like the F-100 Super Sabre and F-84 Thunderstreak with the ordnance-carrying capacity and electronic sophistication that was taken many steps further with advances that were built into aircraft like the F-111 and A-6 from the outset. As a fighter it could be deployed for air defense, as it was on several occasions in Spain and Japan, and in Vietnam it earned a record against MiGs that rivaled for a time that of the F-4 Phantom II. The success of its M61 Vulcan 20mm cannon in almost all those engagements was a major influence in the reintroduction of the gun for fighter-bombers, including the F-4, after a period when "missiles only" was the dominant philosophy.

The F-105's internal nuclear bomb bay was an innovation for attack fighters that was continued into the F-111, but in combat both aircraft carried their considerable load of conventional ordnance externally. Although F-105s' ordnance would be dropped with commendable accuracy, in wartime up to half would fall outside the intended CEP (circular error of probability) at a target. The F-111's navigation/attack systems benefited enormously from the experience of ground mapping and Doppler radar, adding terrain-following capability to the F-105's terrain-avoidance mode and greater accuracy via laser-guided ordnance and better radar.

The pioneering work done by Ryan's Raiders in two-seat F-105Fs established tactics for later Wild Weasel operations in which cockpit teamwork and employment of increasingly complex SEAD (suppression of enemy air defense) electronics were paramount. This tradition was expanded by crews flying the follow-on F-4G Phantom II and EF-111A Raven that were so vital in Operation *Desert Storm*, and the need for specialist Wild Weasel-type aircraft is still a basic element in modern airpower.

The F-105 survived regular over-loading and over-stressing in combat. It was tough enough to bring its crews home despite extreme damage, and, apart from its requirement for strategic bomber-length runways, it was the USAF's best attack aircraft of the 1960s. In the skies over Vietnam it earned a reputation that made it a more-than-worthy successor to its World War II "grandfather," the P-47 Thunderbolt.

FURTHER READING

For additional information on this aircraft the following are recommended:
Anderton, David, *Republic F-105 Thunderchief*, Osprey Air Combat (1983)
Basel, Gene I., *Pak Six*, Associated Creative Writers (1982)
Bell, Kenneth, *100 Missions North*, Brassey's (1993)
Bendell, Anthony "Bugs," *Never in Anger*, Orion Books (1998)
Breuninger, Michael S., *United States Combat Aircrew Survival Equipment*, Schiffer Publishing (1995)
Broughton, Jacksel M., *Rupert Red Two – A Fighter Pilot's Life*, Zenith Press (2007)
Broughton, Jacksel M., *Thud Ridge*, J. B. Lippincott (1969) / Crecy Publishing Ltd (2006)
Broughton, Jacksel M., *Going Downtown*, Orion Books (1988)
Campbell, J., and Hill, M., *Roll-Call Thud*, Schiffer Publishing (1996)
Clodfelter, Mark, *The Limits of Air Power*, The Free Press/Simon and Schuster (1989)
Davies, Peter E., *F-105 Wild Weasel vs SA-2 "Guideline" SAM*, Osprey Duel 35 (2011)
Davies, Peter E., *F-105 Thunderchief Units of the Vietnam War*, Osprey Combat Aircraft (2010)
Davis, Larry, *Wild Weasel – The SAM Suppression Story*, Squadron/Signal Publications (1986)
Davis, Larry and Menard, David, *Republic F-105 Thunderchief*, Specialty Press Publishers (1998)
Drendel, Lou, *Thud*, Squadron/Signal Publications (1986)
Futrell, R. Frank, et al., *Aces and Aerial Victories*, Air University and Office of Air Force History (1976)
Geer, James, *The Republic F-105 Thunderchief, Wing and Squadron Histories*, Schiffer (2002)
Gunston, William T., *Fighters of the Fifties*, Patrick Stephens (1981)
Gunston, William T., *Early Supersonic Fighters of the West*, Ian Allan Ltd (1976)